CONTENTS

INTRODUCTION

This book has been written and designed specifically for the new AQA GCSE Physical Education specification introduced for first teaching in September 2016.

First examination for AQA GCSE Physical Education (8582) is in 2018.

To view the full specification, and examples of assessment material, for AQA GCSE Physical Education, please visit AQA's website: www.aqa.org.uk. The content of this book covers topics in the new specification.

How to use this book

Each chapter has a range of features which have been designed to present the course content in a clear and accessible way, to give you confidence and to support you in your revision and assessment preparation.

Chapter objectives

Each chapter starts with a clear list of what is to be studied.

✔ Check your understanding

These questions have been designed specifically to help to check that you have understood different topics.

Rapid recall

These contain hints and ideas to help you to remember things.

Activity

Activities appear throughout the book and have been designed to help you develop your understanding of various topics.

Key terms

Key terms in **bold** in the text are defined.

Study hints

These are suggestions to help you increase your knowledge of this subject.

PRACTICE QUESTIONS

These are practice questions to help you get used to the type of questions you may encounter in the exam.

Summary

These boxes contain summaries of what you have learned in each section.

Chapter 1a Applied anatomy and physiology

Chapter objectives
- Understand the structure and functions of the skeleton
- Understand the structure and functions of synovial joints
- Understand the movements involved at different joints

The structure and functions of the musculo-skeletal system

Structure of the skeleton

▲ The skeleton provides the framework for our bodies.

The skeletal system provides a framework for the muscular system to produce movement.

1 The skeletal system allows movement at a joint.
2 The shape and type of the bones determine the amount of movement – short bones enable finer controlled movements, long bones enable gross movement.
3 The flat bones protect vital organs.
4 The different joint types allow different types of movement.
5 The skeleton provides a point of attachment for muscles – when muscles contract they pull the bone.

▲ The skeleton protects several vital organs from damage when playing contact sports such as rugby.

▲ The skeleton provides the attachment points for muscles so this gymnast can perform complex movements.

Key terms

Support Bones keep us upright and hold muscles and organs in place.

Protection Some bones surround and protect vital organs from damage.

Long bones The bones of the legs and arms. Long bones support the weight of the body and help with gross movements.

Movement Muscles contract to pull the bones of the skeleton.

The functions of the skeleton

1 **Support** – the bones are solid and rigid. They keep us upright and hold the rest of the body – the muscles and organs – in place.

2 **Protection** – certain parts of the skeleton enclose and protect the body's organs from external forces, e.g. the brain is inside the cranium, the ribs protect the heart and lungs. This function is especially important in activities that involve contact, such as rugby or boxing.

3 **Movement** – the skeleton helps the body move by providing anchor points for the muscles to pull against. The long bones in the arms and legs work as levers to allow certain movements.

4 **Structural shape and points for attachment** – the skeleton gives us our general shape such as height and build. Tall people have long leg bones and larger vertebrae. People with a heavy build have larger clavicles and scapula as well as bigger pelvises. The skeleton also provides anchorage points for the muscles to attach, so when they contract we move.

5 **Mineral storage** – bone stores several minerals, including calcium and phosphorus, which can be released into the blood when needed.

6 **Blood cell production** – the inner marrow of the long bones and ribs produces red and white blood cells. Red blood cells are important in activities because they carry oxygen to the working muscles. White blood cells are important to fight off infections in order to keep healthy.

▲ The skeleton gives shape for both the very tall basketball player and the very heavy sumo wrestler.

Rapid recall

Create an acronym for the functions of the skeleton:
Support, Shape, Protection, Movement, Mineral storage, Production
– e.g. **S**uper **S**tar **P**erformers **M**ake **M**ince **P**ies

Synovial joints

Synovial joints are the most common type of joint in the body.

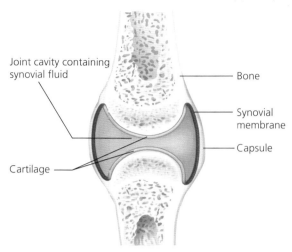

Joint cavity containing synovial fluid

Bone

Synovial membrane

Capsule

Cartilage

▲ Internal structure of a synovial joint.

Synovial joints are characterised by having a fluid-filled space between smooth **cartilage** pads at the end of the bones that form the joint. Surrounding the joint is a tough joint **capsule** that is lined with a **synovial membrane**.

The outer layer of capsule often includes **ligaments** that join bones to bones and strengthen the joint to prevent unnecessary movements and possible **dislocations**. The synovial membrane lining the capsule produces an oily **synovial fluid** that lubricates the joint and reduces friction and wear.

In addition to the joint capsule and ligaments that support a synovial joint, there are several important structures surrounding the joint that help cushion and protect the joint from friction and outside forces. Small bags of synovial fluid, known as **bursae**, surround the joint to reduce the friction from movement of **tendons** across the surface of the joint.

There are many different classes of synovial joints in the body, including hinge joints and ball and socket joints.

> ✔ **Check your understanding**
>
> 1 Explain how different parts of a synovial joint provide support to stabilise the joint.
> 2 Explain how different parts of a synovial joint help it to move freely.
> 3 What is the function of tendons?
> Answers are on page 167.

Key terms

Red blood cells Carry oxygen to muscles.

White blood cells Fight infections.

> **Check your understanding**
>
> 1 What do we need support for?
> 2 What does the skeleton produce?
> 3 How do muscles cause movement?
> Answers are on page 167.

Key terms

Joint Place where two or more bones meet.

Synovial joint Type of joint commonly found in the limbs; contains a **synovial membrane** that produces synovial fluid.

Cartilage Covers ends of bones providing a smooth, friction-free surface.

Synovial fluid Produced by the synovial membrane to lubricate the joint.

Capsule Tough fibrous tissue – surrounds synovial joints; usually supported by ligaments.

Ligaments Join bone to bone.

Dislocation When the bones of a joint separate from their normal position.

Bursae Fluid-filled bag that helps reduce friction in a joint.

Tendon Attaches muscles to bones.

PRACTICE QUESTIONS

1. What are the main functions of ligaments? (1 mark)
2. What is the main function of cartilage? (1 mark)
3. What is the main function of the synovial membrane? (1 mark)

Answers are on page 167.

Activity

Describe the function of each of the following parts of a synovial joint:
- Cartilage
- Capsule
- Synovial membrane
- Synovial fluid
- Bursae

Answers are on page 167.

Key terms

Hinge joint Joint that allows flexion and extension.

Flexion Movement where angle between bones reduces.

Extension Movement where angle between bones increases.

Vertebrae Bones that form the spine or backbone.

Bones that form joints

A joint is where two or more bones are attached for the purpose of motion of body parts.

The head-neck joint

There is a joint where the neck meets the head. The bones in the neck are the **vertebrae**, and the uppermost of these joins with the cranium. This joint allows a person to nod their head.

The elbow joint

▲ The elbow joint is where three bones, the humerus, ulna and radius, meet.

The elbow joint is a complex **hinge joint** formed between the end of the humerus in the upper arm and the ends of the ulna and radius in the forearm.

The inner side of the end of the humerus forms a hinge joint with the ulna, while the outer side meets the end of the head of the radius. The meeting of the humerus, radius and ulna at the elbow allows the lower arm to bend and straighten in relation to the upper arm.

The correct term for the bending at the elbow is **flexion**. Flexion is defined as a movement where the angle between the bone of a joint is reducing. Straightening of the lower arm in relation to the upper arm is called **extension**. Extension is defined as a movement where the angle between the bones of a joint is increasing.

Several ligaments surround the elbow joint which help the joint maintain its stability, allowing movement while resisting dislocation of the bones.

▲ The elbow joint is a hinge joint, moving just like the hinge on a door – forwards and backwards.

The shoulder joint

▲ The shoulder joint is the joint between the humerus and the scapula.

▲ The ball at the end of the humerus fits loosely into the socket of the scapula.

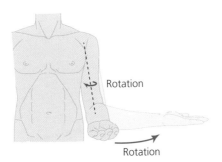

▲ The wide range of movement of the shoulder joint allows for flexion, extension, adduction, abduction and rotation.

Ball and socket joint Joint that allows many movements – flexion and extension; abduction and adduction; and rotation.

Range of movement A measure of the flexibility of a joint in terms of the different movements allowed.

Abduction Movement where limbs are moved away from the body.

Adduction Movement where limbs are moved back towards the body.

Rotation Turning a limb along its long axis.

Pelvis

Femur

▲ The hip joint is formed between the femur and the pelvis.

The shoulder joint is a **ball and socket joint**. It has the greatest **range of movement** of any joint in the body – only ball and socket joints can move forwards and backwards, side to side and rotate around their axis.

Imagine standing upright with your hands by your side. The ball and socket joint at the shoulder can allow your arm to move forwards and backwards – flexion and extension; move away to the side of the body and back again – **abduction** and **adduction**; and enable the arm to **rotate** – turn your thumb in towards the centre of your body or turn it away from the centre of your body.

> ### Rapid recall
>
> When you **add**uct the arm, you 'add' it to the side of the body.

However, the big drawback of a ball and socket joint is that its extensive range of movement makes it more likely to dislocate than other, less mobile synovial joints.

The shoulder joint is formed from two bones, the humerus and the scapula. The round head of the humerus forms a ball and socket joint with a cup-like depression of the scapula.

The joint is held together by ligaments and muscles, but the joint is vulnerable to dislocations from sudden jerks of the arm.

Chest joints

When breathing (see Chapter 1b) the chest cavity changes size because of the action of the breathing muscles. To allow that movement to happen there are joints between the ribs and the sternum, and the ribs and the vertebrae.

The hip joint

The hip joint forms where the femur meets the pelvis. The head of the femur fits into a depression in the pelvis called the acetabulum and forms a ball and socket joint (like the shoulder), which allows the leg to move in several different directions.

The main movements of the hip that occur in sport are flexion and extension. Hip flexion involves the femur moving forwards from a standing position and extension occurs when the femur returns to a standing position.

Flexion

Extension

▲ Flexion and extension at the hip.

The knee joint

▲ The front of the knee joint showing the strong ligaments that help hold the joint in place.

▲ The knee joint is formed from the femur and the tibia.

> **Activity**
>
> Describe the direction of each of the following movements that can happen at the shoulder joint:
> - Flexion
> - Extension
> - Abduction
> - Adduction
> - Rotation
>
> Answers are on page 168.

The knee joint allows the lower leg to move relative to the upper leg while supporting the body's weight. Movements at the knee joint are essential to many everyday activities, including walking, running and moving into a standing position.

The knee is a **hinge joint** formed between two bones: the femur and tibia. The patella lies in front of the femur and is the bone we feel at the front of the knee. It is not actually part of the knee joint.

Between the femur and tibia is a layer of tough, rubbery cartilage known as the **meniscus**, which is the cartilage that is often talked about when describing knee injuries. The meniscus acts as a shock absorber inside the knee to prevent the collision of the leg bones during strenuous activities such as running and jumping.

Many strong ligaments surround the knee to reinforce its structure and hold its bones in place. Two internal ligaments – the anterior and posterior **cruciate ligaments** – also help to keep the bones of the knee in their correct positions, and again are well-known to sportspeople as they are often damaged.

As the knee is a hinge joint, its function is to permit the flexion and extension of the lower leg relative to the thigh.

Study hint

Be aware of questions that ask you to explain about joints – this means you will need to provide a reason, e.g. 'Explain the movement of the shoulder joint' means say how it moves and say why it moves in that way.

Key terms

Meniscus Cartilage acting as a shock absorber between the tibia and femur in the knee joint.

Cruciate ligaments Attach tibia to femur in the knee joint.

✔ Check your understanding

1 Name the bones that form the elbow joint.
2 Which type of synovial joint allows the greatest range of movement? Give an example.
3 What movements are possible at the ankle joint?

Answers are on page 167.

Key terms

Plantar flexion Movement at ankle where the toes are pointed towards the ground.

Dorsiflexion Movement at ankle where the toes are pulled up towards the knee.

Rapid recall

Plantar flexion involves **p**ointing the toes.

The ankle joint

▲ The ankle joint is formed from the tibia and fibula of the lower leg and the talus bone in the foot.

The ankle joint is formed by the lower leg bones – the tibia and fibula – and the talus bone of the foot. These three bones form a synovial **hinge joint**.

The ankle works as a hinge joint, but the forward and backward movements have special names.

Plantar flexion is the term used for the movement that describes the pointing of the foot towards the ground, as in standing on tiptoes.

Dorsiflexion is the opposite movement, and involves the movement of the foot away from the ground, as in pulling the toes up and walking on one's heels.

▲ The ankle movements of dorsiflexion and plantar flexion.

Numerous ligaments work together to limit extreme movements and dislocations of the ankle joint while providing sufficient flexibility that helps the body walk on uneven surfaces and maintain its balance.

The shoulder, elbow, hip, knee and ankle are all examples of synovial joints.

✔ Check your understanding

1 Name the bones that form the knee joint.
2 Identify three different hinge joints.
3 What movements are possible at the shoulder joint?
Answers are on page 168.

PRACTICE QUESTIONS

1. Explain the difference between plantar flexion and dorsiflexion.

(2 marks)

2. What is the correct term for straightening the knee?

(1 mark)

3. Explain the difference between abduction and adduction.

(2 marks)

Answers are on page 167.

Study hint

Be aware of questions that ask for a specific number of answers, e.g. if the question is 'Name **two** bones in the elbow joint' – it is possible that only your first two answers will be accepted.

Activity

Describe the movements that are possible at each of the following joints:
- Shoulder
- Elbow
- Hip
- Knee
- Ankle

Answers are on page 168.

Summary

- The skeleton provides a framework for movement
- The skeleton has several different functions
- Movements occur when bones move the synovial joint at the shoulder, elbow, hip, knee and ankle
- The movements are caused by various muscles pulling these bones

Chapter 1b The structure and function of the cardio-respiratory system

Chapter objectives

- Understand the pathway of air into and out of the lungs
- Understand gas exchange at the alveoli and the features that assist in gaseous exchange
- Understand the structure and function of arteries, capillaries and veins
- Understand the structure of the heart
- Understand the order of the cardiac cycle and the pathway of the blood through the heart
- Understand the terms cardiac output, stroke volume and heart rate, and the relationship between them
- Understand the mechanics of breathing as the interaction of the intercostal muscles, ribs and diaphragm
- Understand and interpret lung volumes through spirometer traces

The respiratory system

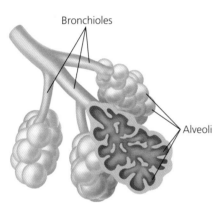

▲ Structure of alveoli.

▲ The respiratory system.

Activity

Draw a single vertical line; draw two lines branching off the bottom of this vertical line, rather like an upside-down Y; draw numerous branches off the ends of the λ. Label these lines as if they were the following parts of the respiratory system:

Trachea

Bronchi

Bronchioles

Answer is on page 170.

When we breathe in, air moves through the mouth and nose and then travels into the trachea. The trachea carries air from the throat to the **lungs**.

The inner surface of the trachea is covered in tiny hairs called cilia, which catch particles of dust, which are then removed when coughing. The trachea is kept open by rings of cartilage.

Near the lungs, the trachea divides into two tubes called **bronchi**, one entering the left and the other entering the right lung. Once inside the lung the bronchi split several ways, forming smaller and smaller bronchi.

The small bronchi further divide into **bronchioles**, which are very narrow tubes, less than 1 millimetre in diameter. There is no cartilage within the bronchioles. At the end of each bronchiole are openings to the **alveoli**. There are usually several alveoli coming from one bronchiole, forming a little clump that resembles a cluster of grapes.

The basic function of alveoli is the exchange of gases. Capillaries carrying blood surround the alveoli. The exchange of oxygen from the lungs into the blood, and the exchange of carbon dioxide in the blood from these capillaries occur through the walls of the alveoli.

Gaseous exchange

Gaseous exchange at the lungs takes place by diffusion. The gases carbon dioxide and oxygen move down a concentration gradient from a high concentration to low concentration.

This means that the oxygen in the alveoli that is at a relatively high concentration diffuses into the blood capillaries where the oxygen concentration is lower. The oxygen that diffuses out of the alveoli is replaced from the air that we continue to breathe in.

The same thing happens in the case of carbon dioxide. Blood in the capillaries surrounding the alveoli contains a relatively high concentration of carbon dioxide and the alveoli contain a lower concentration. Thus, carbon dioxide diffuses into the alveoli from the blood and is eventually breathed out.

Activity

Copy the diagram.

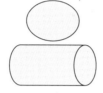

Label the circle as an alveolus and the tube as a blood capillary. Use arrows to show which direction (a) oxygen and (b) carbon dioxide move during breathing.

Explain why the gases move in the directions they do, using the terms **diffusion** and **concentration**.

Answer is on page 170.

Key terms

Trachea (or windpipe) Carries air from the mouth and nose to the lungs.

Bronchi Carries air from the trachea into the lungs.

Bronchioles Carriy air from the bronchi to the alveoli.

Lungs Pair of large, spongy organs optimised for gas exchange between our blood and the air.

Alveoli Many tiny air sacs in the lungs which allow for rapid gaseous exchange.

PRACTICE QUESTION

Name the structures that air moves through as it passes from the mouth to the alveoli.

(3 marks)

Answer is on page 169.

▲ Gaseous exchange.

✔ Check your understanding

1 What is the function of cilia?
2 What is the difference between bronchi and bronchioles?
3 What is the function of the rings of cartilage in the trachea?
4 What is the function of the alveoli?

Answers are on page 168.

PRACTICE QUESTION

Describe the process of diffusion that occurs in the lungs. (2 marks)

Answer is on page 169.

Key terms

Haemoglobin The red pigment found in red blood cells.

Oxyhaemoglobin Formed when oxygen combines with haemoglobin.

Activity

List four factors that assist rapid diffusion; then reduce each factor to a single term. Produce and learn an acronym for those four factors.

Answer is on page 170.

✔ Check your understanding

1 Explain why oxygen diffuses into the blood.
2 Name four factors that assist gas exchange.
3 What is the function of haemoglobin?

Answers are on page 168.

Rapid recall

INspiration is breathing **IN**.

Rapid recall

The **IN**tercostal muscles **IN**crease the volume of the chest cavity.

The process of diffusion is a passive process and is helped by several factors:

● The alveoli are very small in size and large in number (there are millions in each lung), and so the alveoli provide a large surface area for the exchange of gases.
● The surface of alveoli and the walls of the blood capillaries are very thin (one cell thick) and moist which also helps the exchange of gases.
● The alveoli and capillaries are touching each other so there is a very short distance for diffusion (short diffusion pathway).
● Each alveolus is surrounded by a network of blood capillaries, so there is a rich supply of blood for the gases to diffuse into/from.

When diffusing into the blood, the oxygen combines with **haemoglobin**, forming **oxyhaemoglobin**. Haemoglobin is a red pigment that is found in red blood cells. It is the haemoglobin in red blood cells that transports oxygen around the body. Carbon dioxide is also carried in red blood cells combined with haemoglobin.

Breathing

Breathing is a two-stage process. **Inspiration** (inhalation) is the intake of air into the lungs, which is brought about by increasing the volume of the chest cavity. **Expiration** (exhalation) is the expulsion of air from the lungs through reducing the volume of the chest cavity.

Both inspiration and expiration involve the use of muscles, the diaphragm and intercostal muscles. When these muscles contract they cause the chest cavity to increase in size and therefore increase its volume.

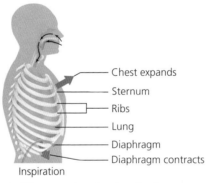
Chest expands
Sternum
Ribs
Lung
Diaphragm
Diaphragm contracts
Inspiration

▲ Diagram showing inspiration.

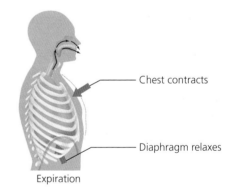
Chest contracts
Diaphragm relaxes
Expiration

▲ Diagram showing expiration.

During inspiration the breathing muscles contract. Contraction of the dome-shaped diaphragm causes it to flatten, thus enlarging the chest cavity. At the same time, contraction of the intercostal muscles causes the ribs to rise, thus also increasing the size of the chest cavity.

When the chest cavity expands, its volume increases. This reduces the pressure in the chest cavity and air is passively drawn into the lungs. Air passes from the higher pressure outside the lungs to the lower pressure inside the lungs.

During expiration the breathing muscles relax. The diaphragm curves and returns to its dome shape; the weight of the ribs causes them to descend and the chest volume decreases. The reduction in the size of the chest cavity increases the pressure of the air in the lungs and causes it to be expelled. Expiration is passive; the breathing muscles simply relax. Air passes from the high pressure in the lungs to the low pressure in the bronchi and trachea.

During exercise, the active process of inspiration is assisted by the additional contraction of the pectoral and sternocleidomastoid muscles, which further increase the size of the chest cavity and so allow more air to enter the lungs.

Also during exercise, the normally passive process of expiration is assisted by contraction of the **abdominal muscles**, which help force air out of the lungs and so speed up expiration.

Lung volumes

A spirometer is a piece of apparatus designed to measure lung volumes. It consists of a chamber filled with oxygen that floats on a tank of water. A person breathes from a mouthpiece attached to a tube connected to the chamber.

Breathing in takes oxygen away from the chamber, which then sinks down. Breathing out then pushes air into the chamber causing it to float. During these movements, the lung volumes involved may be seen and measured.

The lung volumes are the amount of air breathed in, breathed out and found within the lungs at any given time.

Tidal Volume is the amount of air that enters the lungs during normal inspiration at rest. The average tidal volume is 500 ml. The same amount leaves the lungs during expiration.

The **Inspiratory Reserve Volume** is the amount of extra air inspired (above tidal volume) during a deep breath in. This can be as high as 3000 ml.

The **Expiratory Reserve Volume** is the amount of extra air expired (above tidal volume) during a forceful breath out.

Residual Volume is the amount of air left in the lungs following a maximal expiration. There is always some air remaining in the lungs.

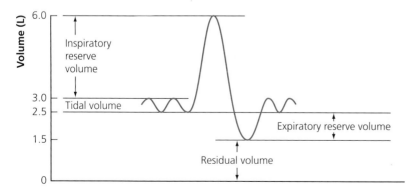

▲ Typical spirometer trace.

Check your understanding

1 Name the breathing muscles used to inspire air during rest.
2 Name the breathing muscles used to inspire air during exercise.
3 How is air expired during rest?
4 Name the breathing muscles used to expire air during exercise.

Answers are on page 168.

PRACTICE QUESTIONS

1. Describe the mechanics of inhalation at rest. (2 marks)
2. Describe how the mechanics of breathing change during exercise. (2 marks)

Answer is on page 169.

Study hint

Remember to avoid abbreviations such as TV, IRV or ERV. Write them out in full.

Key terms

Abdominal muscles The muscles which help force air out of the lungs and so speed up expiration.

Tidal volume The volume of air breathed in (or out) during a normal breath at rest.

Expiratory reserve volume (ERV) The additional air that can be forcibly exhaled after the expiration of a normal tidal volume.

Inspiratory reserve volume (IRV) The additional air that can be forcibly inhaled after the inspiration of a normal tidal volume.

Residual volume The volume of air that remains in the lungs after a maximal expiration.

PRACTICE QUESTION

While running, a performer will experience changes in lung volumes. Complete the table below to show how the tidal volume, inspiratory reserve volume and expiratory reserve volume change during exercise. (3 marks)

Volume name	Value at rest	Change during exercise
Breathing rate	16 breaths/min	Increases
Tidal volume	500 cm³	
Inspiratory reserve volume	3100 cm³	
Expiratory reserve volume	1200 cm³	
Residual volume	1100 cm³	No change

Answers are on page 169.

Activity

Copy the following diagram and label the tidal volume, the inspiratory reserve volume, the expiratory reserve volume and the residual volume.

Answers are on page 170.

Blood vessels

✔ Check your understanding

1 What is the tidal volume?
2 Which lung volume is used to increase the amount of air breathed in?
3 What is the name of the amount of air left in the lungs after a full expiration?

Answers are on page 169.

Artery

Vein

Capillary

▲ Blood is carried around the body in blood vessels. There are different types of blood vessel, each having a different function.

Arteries carry blood away from the heart. The blood within arteries is under the highest pressure. Arteries are elastic; they maintain the blood pressure by recoiling and narrowing when the heart is relaxing. Small arteries have muscular walls that can adjust their diameter to increase or decrease blood flow to a particular part of the body. The rings of muscle in the small arteries can contract. This makes the diameter of those arteries smaller and reduces the flow of blood through that artery. This is called **vasoconstriction**. The diameter of the small arteries can also increase (causing **vasodilation**) to allow more blood to flow through that artery to the tissues. Vasodilation occurs during exercise to allow more blood to flow to the exercising muscles.

Capillaries are tiny, thin-walled blood vessels that join arteries (which carry blood away from the heart) and **veins** (which carry blood back to the heart). The thin walls of the capillaries allow gas exchange – oxygen to pass from the blood into tissues and carbon dioxide to pass from tissues into the blood. Nutrients also diffuse from blood in capillaries into the surrounding tissues and waste products diffuse from the tissues into the blood.

Blood flows from the capillaries into very small veins, then into larger veins that lead back to the heart. Veins have much thinner walls than arteries, because the blood pressure in veins is much lower. They also have a large internal diameter (lumen). Veins have valves to prevent blood from flowing backwards.

Key terms

Artery Blood vessel carrying blood away from the heart.

Vein Blood vessel carrying blood towards the heart.

Capillaries Very thin blood vessels that allow gas exchange to happen.

Vasoconstriction Reducing the diameter of small arteries to reduce blood flow to tissues.

Vasodilation Increasing the diameter of small arteries to increase blood flow to tissues.

Rapid recall

Remember – **A**rteries carry blood **A**way from the heart.

▼ Differences between functions of arteries, capillaries and veins

ARTERIES	CAPILLARIES	VEINS
Carry blood away from the heart	Huge network of tiny vessels linking arteries and veins	Carry blood towards the heart
Most (but not all) arteries carry bright red oxygenated blood	Very narrow – only one red blood cell at a time	Most (but not all) veins carry dark red deoxygenated blood
Stretch as blood surges through and then return to normal shape – they have a pulse	Very thin walls (one cell thick) to allow rapid diffusion of substances into and out of the blood	No stretch; no pulse
Thick, muscular and elastic walls to withstand pressure		Thin-walled
Small lumen (internal diameter)		Large lumen (internal diameter)
		Have valves to prevent backflow of blood

✔ Check your understanding

1 What is the function of the elastic tissue in arteries?
2 Which type of blood vessel contains valves?
3 What is vasodilation?
4 Why are capillaries thin-walled?

Answers are on page 169.

Activity

Draw a square and divide it into four quarters. Use this as a simple diagram of the heart. Label the right and left atria and the right and left ventricles on your diagram.

Answer is on page 171.

Activity

Use the same diagram from the activity above. Colour the left side of the heart blue to represent deoxygenated blood. Colour the right side of the heart red to represent oxygenated blood.

Use arrows to show the direction of flow of the blood into and out of the different heart chambers.

Answer is on page 171.

Key terms

Atria Upper chambers of the heart that collect blood from veins.

Ventricles Lower chambers of the heart which pump blood out of the heart to the arteries.

Cardiac cycle Sequence of events that occur when the heart beats.

Systole Term used to describe the contraction phase of the cardiac cycle.

Diastole Term used to describe the relaxation phase of the cardiac cycle.

Structure of the heart

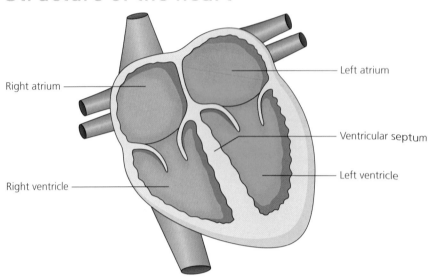

Right atrium

Left atrium

Ventricular septum

Left ventricle

Right ventricle

▲ Structure of the heart.

The heart is a muscular organ about the size of a closed fist that pumps blood around the body. It is divided into separate left and right sides, and each side has an upper and a lower chamber. The upper chambers are the **atria**, which collect blood from veins, and the lower chambers are the **ventricles**, which pump out blood through the arteries.

The right side of the heart takes in deoxygenated blood through the veins and delivers it to the lungs for oxygenation. The oxygenated blood returns from the lungs to the left side of the heart and is then pumped into various arteries that provide oxygen and nutrients to the body tissues by transporting the blood throughout the body.

Cardiac cycle

The cardiac cycle is the sequence of events that occurs when the heart beats. There are two phases of the cardiac cycle. In **diastole**, the heart ventricles are relaxed and the heart fills with blood. In the **systole**, the ventricles contract and pump blood to the arteries. One cardiac cycle is completed when the heart fills with blood and the blood is pumped out of the heart.

The events of the cardiac cycle described below trace the path of the blood as it enters the right side of the heart, is pumped to the lungs, travels back to the left side of the heart and is pumped out to the rest of the body. It should be noted that both the left and right sides of the heart go through diastole and systole at the same time.

The flow of blood through the heart is controlled by pressure changes that cause different valves in the heart to open to allow blood to flow, and at other times close to prevent backflow of blood.

During diastole, the atria and ventricles are relaxed and the valves between the atria and ventricles (atrioventricular valves) are open. Deoxygenated blood from the main veins, the vena cavae, flows into the right atrium. The open atrioventricular valves allow blood to pass through to the ventricles.

Systole then occurs and the right atrium begins to contract, emptying its contents into the right ventricle. The right ventricle contracts soon after, forcing blood out of the heart along the pulmonary artery towards the lungs. The right atrioventricular valve is forced closed and prevents the blood from flowing back into the right atrium.

The deoxygenated blood flows through the pulmonary arteries to the lungs where gas exchange occurs. The blood picks up oxygen, and carbon dioxide is removed before the blood returns to the left atrium of the heart through the pulmonary veins.

The oxygenated blood from the pulmonary veins fills the left atrium during diastole. Systole then begins again and the left atrium empties its contents into the left ventricle.

During systole, the left ventricle contracts, forcing the left atrioventricular valve to close, and the oxygenated blood is pumped into the aorta.

Cardiac output

Cardiac output is the volume of blood that the heart is able to pump out. It is usually measured in litres per minute.

The cardiac output represents the volume of oxygenated blood that is delivered to the body.

Two major factors form the cardiac output – the heart rate, which is the number of times the heart beats each minute, and the stroke volume, which is the volume of blood that leaves the heart during each contraction.

Increasing the heart rate increases the cardiac output by increasing the number of volumes of blood released into the system. The heart rate increases usually before activity because of the expectation of exercise. This slight increase in heart rate before exercise is called the anticipatory rise.

The stroke volume can be increased by the heart contracting with more force and so pushing more blood out with each beat.

The cardiac output, heart rate and stroke volume are related such that:

Cardiac Output [Q] = Heart Rate [HR] × Stroke Volume [SV]

✔ Check your understanding

1 What is the cardiac output?
2 What is the relationship between stroke volume, heart rate and cardiac output?
3 What is the stroke volume?
4 What is the cardiac output of a performer who has a stroke volume of 70 mls and a heart rate of 70 beats per minute?

Answers are on page 169.

✔ Check your understanding

1 Distinguish between systole and diastole.
2 What is the function of the heart (atrioventricular) valves?
3 Describe the passage of blood from the right atrium to the lungs.
4 Describe the passage of blood from the lungs to the left ventricle.

Answers are on page 169.

PRACTICE QUESTION

Describe the passage of blood from it leaving the right atria to it eventually reaching the left ventricle.   (4 marks)

Answer is on page 169.

Study hint

If you have to provide mathematical information, remember to include the units – possibly converting mls/min into L/min.

PRACTICE QUESTION

Briefly explain the terms 'cardiac output' and 'stroke volume' and the relationship between them.   (3 marks)

Answer is on page 169.

Summary

- Different structures are involved in the pathway of air into and out of the lungs
- Gas exchange in the alveoli is assisted by several features
- Blood vessels have structures that suit their function
- The cardiac cycle consists of systole and diastole and forces blood through the different parts of the heart
- There is a relationship between cardiac output, stroke volume and heart rate
- Different muscles cause changes in the volume and pressures within the chest cavity during breathing
- A spirometer may be used to measure different lung volumes

Chapter 1c Anaerobic and aerobic exercise

Chapter objectives

- Understand the idea of aerobic and anaerobic exercise during differing intensities
- Understand the recovery process from vigorous exercise in terms of Excess Post-exercise Oxygen Consumption (EPOC)/ oxygen debt
- Understand methods to help recover from strenuous exercise
- Understand the immediate effects of exercise (during exercise)
- Understand the short-term effects of exercise (24 to 36 hours after exercise)
- Understand the long-term effects of exercise (months and years of exercising)

Exercise

When somebody exercises they need to supply energy for muscle contractions. This energy is usually supplied by breaking down food (mainly glucose) using oxygen – because this process uses oxygen it is called **aerobic exercise**.

Aerobic exercise occurs at low to moderate levels of exertion, when energy can be produced using oxygen. Walking and jogging are good examples of exercises where the energy for muscle contractions is provided aerobically.

Anaerobic exercise is where the energy needed for the exercise is provided in the absence of oxygen. Sprinting and shot putting are examples of activities where the energy is provided anaerobically.

The main difference between aerobic and anaerobic exercises is the intensity and the duration of the exercise involved.

Aerobic activities involve relatively gentle exercises that can be maintained for a long period of time. Aerobic activities are those where normal breathing can be used to supply the oxygen needed to the working muscles.

Rapid recall

Aerobic sounds like 'air'; air contains oxygen.

Anaerobic activities involve very high intensity actions that can only be continued for a short period of time. Anaerobic exercises, if continued, will leave you breathless.

There are some activities, such as team games, that contain a mixture of aerobic and anaerobic exercise. During team games there will be times when the exercise is relatively gentle and the performer is walking/

Rapid recall

If you're asked for examples of aerobic and/or anaerobic exercise, use marathon running for aerobic exercise and sprinting for anaerobic exercise.

▲ Jogging is an aerobic exercise.

Key terms

Aerobic exercise In the presence of/using oxygen.

Anaerobic exercise In the absence of enough/without oxygen.

▲ Sprinting is an anaerobic exercise.

Activity

Separate the following list of sports into mainly aerobic exercises, anaerobic exercises and mixed exercises:

Netball, Pole vault, Marathon, Trampolining, Cricket, Triathlon.

Answer is on page 172.

▲ Team games involve a mixture of aerobic and anaerobic exercises.

Activity

Identify three aerobic and three anaerobic movements/actions from a team game of your choice.

Answer is on page 173.

▲ Exercise may cause fatigue.

Key terms

Lactic acid Waste product from anaerobic exercise.

Oxygen debt Temporary oxygen shortage in the body due to strenuous exercise.

EPOC Increased rate of oxygen intake following strenuous activity.

jogging and is aerobic. At other times the performer may be sprinting and the exercise is strenuous and becomes anaerobic.

Aerobic exercise involves the performer using oxygen to break down foods such as glucose. This reaction provides the energy needed for the activity and produces water and carbon dioxide as waste products. The process may be summarised as:

$$\text{Glucose} + \text{Oxygen} \rightarrow \text{Energy} + \text{Carbon Dioxide} + \text{Water}$$

In anaerobic exercises, no oxygen is used. Because of this, the glucose is not fully broken down to carbon dioxide and water. Instead it is converted into lactic acid while producing the energy needed for the activity. The process may be summarised as:

$$\text{Glucose} \rightarrow \text{Energy} + \text{Lactic Acid}$$

Lactic acid is one of the major causes of fatigue. This is why anaerobic exercises cannot be continued for more than a minute or so. The build-up of lactic acid in muscles causes fatigue and eventually pain and the exercise has to slow down or, if strenuous, stop.

✔ Check your understanding

1 Distinguish between aerobic and anaerobic exercise.
2 Write an equation that summarises aerobic exercise.
3 What is lactic acid?
4 Write an equation that summarises anaerobic exercise.

Answers are on page 171.

PRACTICE QUESTION

Is the marathon an aerobic or anaerobic event? Explain your answer. (3 marks)

Answer is on page 172.

EPOC (Oxygen debt)

During a short, intense burst of exercise such as sprinting, energy is generated anaerobically or without oxygen. When the body works anaerobically it produces energy without oxygen, and instead produces **lactic acid** as a waste product.

When the strenuous exercise stops, the performer will still be breathing heavily.

During this time, after strenuous exercise, the body takes in extra oxygen to 'repay' the **oxygen debt**. The term oxygen debt is more properly known as **EPOC: Excess Post-exercise Oxygen Consumption**.

During recovery after anaerobic exercise, the body needs the extra oxygen to remove the lactic acid produced during the exercise. This is why the performer continues to breathe heavily, to repay his oxygen debt.

How long this oxygen debt lasts depends on how much lactic acid is produced, which in turn depends on how strenuous the exercise was and how long it lasted. It can take several hours to completely remove all the lactic acid produced during very intense exercise.

Activity

Watch a 400 m race on a YouTube clip. Explain in your own words why the performers look so tired after the event and the processes that are occurring during their recovery.

Answers are on page 173.

Answers are on page 173.

Immediate effects of exercise (during exercise)

When a performer begins to exercise, the body has to supply extra oxygen to the working muscles. In order to do that, several changes take place in the body.

First, the heart begins to beat faster. Normal resting heart rate is somewhere around 70 to 80 beats per minute, but can vary considerably. Exercise can easily raise the heart rate to 100–150 beats per minute or even higher, depending on how hard the exercise is.

The heart will also contract more powerfully during exercise, increasing the stroke volume. The increased heart rate and the more powerful contractions mean that more blood is being pumped around the body to supply the muscles with the glucose and oxygen they need.

The second immediate effect of exercise is that the breathing rate increases. The resting breathing rate is about 15 breaths per minute. When exercise begins, not only does breathing rate increase, but so does the depth of breathing, so increasing the tidal volume. The increased rate and depth of breathing allows for greater gaseous exchange at the lungs, so more oxygen enters the blood and more carbon dioxide is breathed out.

The third effect of exercise is that body temperature increases. This is because muscles are contracting more often and this generates heat, which increases body temperature. This increase in temperature is noticeable by the way the body tries to control it and keep cool. The body begins to sweat to try to lose heat by evaporation of sweat off the skin's surface. The skin goes red as blood vessels near the skin's surface open, to try to lose heat by radiation.

Short-term effects of exercise (24 to 36 hours after exercise)

Exercise may also affect the body some time after the exercise has finished. Individuals may suffer from fatigue the day after strenuous exercise. This tiredness is simply caused by the muscles having worked especially hard and becoming swollen with fluids, which leave them feeling heavy. This effect usually passes within a day or two.

Sometimes following an exercise session a performer may feel dizzy and light-headed as if they might faint. This is often caused by low blood sugar or a drop in blood pressure. This is more likely to occur if the performer has sweated heavily.

Nausea is the feeling of sickness or vomiting which can occur during and after exercise. It may be caused by over-exertion during exercise, or

Check your understanding

1 What does EPOC stand for?
2 Why do we get an 'oxygen debt' after strenuous exercise?
3 What is the function of EPOC?

Answers are on page 171.

PRACTICE QUESTION

What is Excess Post-exercise Oxygen Consumption?
(2 marks)

Answer is on page 172.

PRACTICE QUESTION

What are the immediate effects of exercise on the body? (3 marks)

Answer is on page 172.

▲ Sweating is normal during exercise.

Activity

Make a list that summarises the three immediate effects of exercise.

Answer is on page 173.

Study hint
Remember to avoid abbreviations such as DOMS or EPOC unless you have first written the term out in full.

▲ Cramp may result from strenuous exercise and a loss of fluids.

Key terms

DOMS (Delayed Onset Muscle Soreness) The pain/stiffness felt in the days following strenuous exercise.

Nausea Feelings of sickness during/after exercise.

Cramp Involuntary contraction of a muscle.

Activity

Make a list that summarises the four short-term effects of exercise.

Answer is on page 173.

✔ Check your understanding

1 What are the immediate effects of exercise?
2 What are the short-term effects of exercise?
3 What is DOMS?
4 What causes DOMS?

Answers are on page 171.

from ending an exercise session too abruptly. Lack of water intake during exercise is a well-known cause of headaches and nausea during exercise. Exercising at a heavy rate causes blood flow to be taken away from a full stomach, another possible cause of nausea.

The pain and stiffness sometimes felt in muscles after unaccustomed or strenuous exercise is more properly called **delayed onset muscle soreness (DOMS)**. It is caused by eccentric muscle contractions performed during exercise, which causes tiny tears in muscle fibres, leading to swelling. The muscle is supposed to tear, because it repairs stronger, and this is the main benefit of training. Usually the muscle adapts rapidly to prevent muscle damage, and the soreness, if the exercise is repeated.

DOMS is different to, but often confused with, **cramp**. Cramp is a painful involuntary contraction of a muscle that is typically caused by fatigue or strain of the muscle and is often linked to dehydration and loss of minerals due to excessive sweating.

PRACTICE QUESTION

People may suffer when they begin an exercise programme. Explain the causes of:

a) fatigue

b) DOMS   (2 marks)

Answer is on page 172.

The recovery process from vigorous exercise

If undertaking strenuous exercise, the performer will want to avoid the problems of excessive fatigue/tiredness, nausea/light-headedness and DOMS/cramp. There are several precautions that can be taken to help recovery from exercise.

A **cool down** should be undertaken following the exercise. A cool down should consist of 5 to 10 minutes of walking or jogging to help decrease body temperature and remove waste products such as lactic acid from the working muscles. This should be followed by 5 to 10 minutes of static stretching exercises, which will help muscles to relax.

An appropriate cool down has the following benefits:

- aids in the clearing of waste products – including lactic acid
- reduces the potential for DOMS
- reduces the chances of dizziness or fainting caused by the pooling of blood at the extremities
- allows breathing and heart rate to slowly return to their resting rates and so prevent sudden changes in heart rhythm, which could be dangerous.

Rehydration is the process of replacing the fluids that are lost during exercise, mainly through sweating.

Replacement of water on its own is not enough, because the body also loses minerals during sweating and these will need replacing as well. The performer also needs to replace the energy used during the exercise. During both aerobic and anaerobic exercise, glucose is used to produce the energy needed for muscle contractions. This glucose needs replacing. Glucose is a type of carbohydrate and the body will convert any carbohydrates it consumes into glucose. Therefore, it is advisable for the performer to take in extra carbohydrates following strenuous exercise.

These could easily be added to the fluids that are being consumed to replace the water and minerals lost during the exercise. In practical terms, drinks such as flavoured milk or meal-replacement drinks are quite suitable for manipulation of diet following strenuous exercise.

Common sense suggests that consuming large quantities of flavoured milks or meal-replacement drinks while indulging in light rather than strenuous exercise will cause an increase in weight rather than a beneficial effect. This is because it is very rare to exercise sufficiently hard that the amount of energy used is equivalent to that consumed in a meal.

Another method of speeding up recovery after strenuous exercise is to use **ice baths**. The theory behind ice baths is related to the fact that intense exercise actually causes tiny tears in muscle fibres. This muscle damage stimulates the muscles to repair and strengthen themselves, but it is also linked with delayed onset muscle pain and soreness (DOMS), which occurs between 24 and 72 hours after exercise.

▲ Rehydration is important during and after exercise.

▲ Performers use ice baths to prevent DOMS and speed up recovery from exercise.

Key terms

Cool down Undertaken after exercise to speed up recovery – e.g. walking, jogging, followed by static stretches.

Rehydration Replacing lost water, minerals and carbohydrates after exercise.

Ice bath Immersion in cold water to speed up recovery.

Massage The rubbing and kneading of muscles and joints with the hands.

✔ Check your understanding

1. What should be included in a rehydration drink?
2. How do ice baths help prevent DOMS?
3. What are the benefits of a cool down?

Answers are on page 172.

Activity

Make a list of the three different ways that recovery from exercise can be assisted.

Answer is on page 173.

PRACTICE QUESTION

Identify two parts of an effective cool down. (2 marks)

Answer is on page 172.

The ice bath is thought to constrict blood vessels and flush waste products, like lactic acid, out of the affected tissues. They are also supposed to reduce swelling. Both of these factors are thought to cause DOMS.

Then, once the performer is out of the ice bath and the muscles start warming up, there is an increased blood flow through the muscles, which improves the healing process.

Massage, which involves the rubbing and kneading of muscles and joints with the hands, can help reduce the pain that may be caused by too much physical activity. Massage can prevent or relieve delayed onset muscle soreness by encouraging blood flow throughout the body, preventing muscle fatigue. It may also be used to reduce the swelling in muscles that may be causing the fatigue or stiffness in newly exercising muscles.

Long-term effects of exercise (months and years of exercising)

Many of the effects of regular training are not seen for months or even years after training has started. This is because the changes are to the actual structure of the body to allow the various systems of the body to work more efficiently during exercise.

Regular exercise will tend to reduce the weight of the body. This is because fat stores are used to supply the glucose the body needs for energy. As well as that, if the exercise is mainly anaerobic, there will be a tendency to increase the size of the muscles involved in the exercise. This is called hypertrophy. The result of these two factors is that body shape may change.

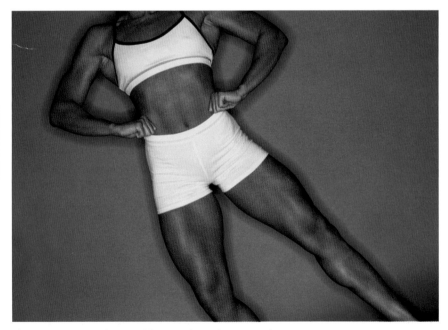

▲ Muscles get bigger with exercise – hypertrophy.

Depending on the type of exercise undertaken, certain components of fitness may be developed. For example, if the exercise is mainly anaerobic and involves moving heavy objects around such as weights, then there will be a build-up of muscle strength.

Similarly, regular exercises that are repeated, such as press-ups or sit-ups will lead to an improvement in muscular endurance in those muscles involved in the movement.

Muscles, tendons and ligaments around joints get stronger and the joints become more stable. At the same time, the repeated movements involving joints means that the suppleness (flexibility) at joints increases.

Exercises that involve rapid anaerobic movements such as sprinting will eventually lead to an increase in speed. Similarly, exercises that involve slower, rhythmical, aerobic movements, such as running or swimming, will eventually build up the performer's cardio-vascular endurance and hence improve their stamina.

Less obvious is the fact that a long-term training programme will mean that the heart is beating at a higher rate than normal for long periods of time. The heart is a muscle, and like any other muscle exposed to regular intense exercise, it will increase in size. In other words, **hypertrophy** of the heart will occur.

This increased size of the heart means that it is able to contract with greater force and pump out more blood with each beat. In other words, the stroke volume of the heart increases because of regular training.

Linked to this hypertrophy of the heart is the fact that there isn't that great a change in the overall size of the body, because the skeleton is the same shape and size, as are all the major organs. Therefore the amount of blood that the body needs when not exercising remains essentially the same.

The amount of blood that the body receives depends on the cardiac output. Remember that:

cardiac output = stroke volume x heart rate

So, at rest, the cardiac output of a hypertrophied heart remains unchanged, but the stroke volume increases because of repeated exercise. This means that the heart rate must reduce to produce the same resting cardiac output. This reduction in resting heart rate in performers who have undertaken months or years of regular training is called **bradycardia**.

✔ Check your understanding

1 Why might body shape change following repeated exercises?
2 Explain the effects of long-term exercise on the heart.
3 In what ways does long-term exercise benefit fitness?

Answers are on page 172.

PRACTICE QUESTIONS

The long-term effects of exercise include the improvement in fitness.

a) Name four fitness components improved by long-term exercise.

b) Suggest three other long-term effects of exercise.   (4 marks)

Answer is on page 172.

Rapid recall

Long-term effects of exercise improve the **four Ss** – speed, stamina, suppleness, strength.

Activity

Use numbers to help understand the idea of bradycardia.

If Q = SV x HR and Q = 12 and SV = 3, then HR must equal ?

If SV increases to 4 and Q remains the same, HR must become ?

Answer is on page 173.

Key terms

Hypertrophy Increase in size of muscles/heart due to long-term exercise.

Bradycardia Lowered resting heart rate due to long-term exercise.

Activity

Make a list of the fitness components (see Chapter 3) improved by repeated exercises and for each one describe the type of exercise that should be undertaken.

Answer is on page 173.

Summary

- Aerobic and anaerobic exercises involve working at different intensities
- Recovery from exercise involves Excess Post-exercise Oxygen Consumption (EPOC)/oxygen debt
- There are different ways to help recover from strenuous exercise
- Exercise has immediate, short-term and long-term effects on the body

Chapter 2 Movement analysis

Levers

A lever is made up of three basic parts. These are the **fulcrum**, an **effort** (also called a force) and a **resistance** (also called the load). The fulcrum is the pivot point of a lever, the effort is the force that is applied to one part of the lever and the resistance is at the other end working against the force of the effort.

There are three classes of levers. A **first class lever** is the simplest.

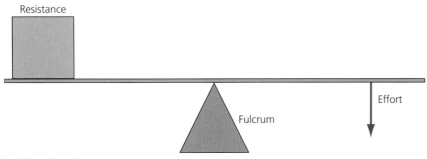

▲ First class lever.

It has the fulcrum lying between the effort and the resistance. An example of a first class lever in the human body is the way the triceps muscle of the arm acts during extension. In this first class lever system, the elbow is the fulcrum and the hand is the load. The effort is applied by the triceps muscle to move the resistance in the hand.

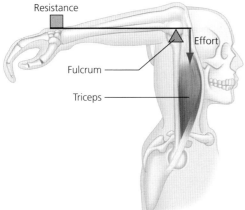

◀ The first class lever system at the elbow joint.

Key terms

Fulcrum The part of a lever system that pivots; joints are the fulcrums in the body's lever systems.

Resistance The load to be moved by a lever system; usually this involves weight when the body's lever systems are involved.

Effort The force applied to move the resistance or weight; in the body, the effort is provided by muscles exerting a force.

First class lever Found at the elbow joint, where the triceps causes extension of the lower arm.

27

Key term

Second class lever Found at the ankle, where the gastrocnemius causes plantar flexion.

▲ The second class lever system at the ankle joint.

Key term

Third class lever The majority of the body's joints act as third class levers; for example, the biceps acting at the elbow to cause flexion acts as a third class lever system.

Rapid recall

It might help you remember the three classes of levers and the corresponding positions of their components if you remember that in levers, the middle component follows the mnemonic:

1, 2, 3 – F, R, E

In other words, in first class levers, the Fulcrum **F** is in the middle; in second class levers, Resistance **R** is in the middle; and in third class levers, Effort **E** is in the middle.

A **second class lever** is one where the fulcrum lies at one end with the effort at the other end. The resistance then lies in the middle of the effort and the fulcrum.

▲ Second class lever.

In the human body, an example would be the ankle joint. The fulcrum is the ball of the foot, with the effort being the contraction of the gastrocnemius muscle. The resistance then would be the weight of the person.

The final class of levers is the **third class lever**. In this kind of lever system, the fulcrum is located at one end and the resistance is at the other end of the lever. The effort is located between the fulcrum and the resistance.

▲ Third class lever.

An example of a third class lever in the human body is with the biceps muscle in the arm acting on the elbow joint to move a resistance in the hand.

▲ The third class lever system at the elbow joint.

Mechanical advantage

Different types of levers have different types of **mechanical advantage** in how they work. The mechanical advantage of different levers depends on the distance between the effort and the fulcrum when compared to the distance of the resistance from the fulcrum. These distances are known as the effort arm and resistance arm respectively.

Mechanical advantage = effort arm divided by the resistance arm

▲ Idea of resistance arm and effort arm.

Key term

Mechanical advantage The benefit to a lever system of having either a short effort arm – giving rapid movements over a large range of movement – or a short resistance arm – giving the advantage of being able to move a heavy weight.

First and third class levers have an effort arm that is much shorter than the resistance arm and therefore the effort arm ÷ the resistance arm is less than one. This arrangement of long effort arm and shorter resistance arm will help speed up the movement of the resistance and produce a wide range of movement. This occurs in the action of the biceps acting on the elbow joint as a third class lever system.

During flexion at the elbow, the effort arm is the distance of the effort (the biceps) from the fulcrum (the elbow joint). The resistance arm is the distance of the hand from the fulcrum (the elbow joint). This allows the hand to move very quickly and through a large range of movement.

The vast majority of joints in the body are third class lever systems, with a short effort arm and long resistance arm. This means that these joints can move very quickly over a large range of movement.

Activity

Draw a diagram to show how the first class lever system operates at the elbow. Include the following terms in your diagram:

- Fulcrum
- Effort
- Resistance
- Triceps
- Elbow joint
- Effort arm
- Resistance arm

Answer is on page 175.

Second class levers such as the ankle joint are able to overcome a large resistance with an effort that is fairly small by comparison because the resistance arm is shorter than the effort arm. This gives a high value for mechanical advantage and therefore the action of the effort (gastrocnemius muscle) can easily move the resistance, which is essentially the weight of the body.

> **Activity**
>
> Draw a diagram to show how the second class lever system operates at the ankle. Include the following terms in your diagram:
> - Fulcrum
> - Effort
> - Resistance
> - Gastrocnemius
> - Ball of foot
> - Effort arm
> - Resistance arm
>
> Answer is on page 176.

> ✔ **Check your understanding**
>
> 1 When running, the knee joint works as a lever system. Name, sketch and label the lever system operating at the knee during running.
> 2 When performing a throw-in during football or rugby, or a chest pass during netball or basketball, the arm straightens at the elbow. Name, sketch and label the lever system operating at the elbow during this type of movement.
> 3 Name, sketch and label the lever system operating at the ankle during running.
> 4 State **two** mechanical advantages of the lever system that is used at the ankle joint.
>
> Answers are on pages 173–174.

Muscle action

Antagonistic muscle action

Muscles can only contract and pull. Therefore, joints have to have two or more muscles working opposite each other, one to pull the bones in one direction and another to pull the bones in the opposite direction.

As one muscle contracts, the second muscle relaxes. As the second muscle contracts, so the first muscle relaxes. This is known as **antagonistic** muscle action.

A good example of this is the upper arm where the triceps and biceps are on opposite sides of the humerus. As the biceps contracts, the lower arm (radius and ulna) moves up towards the shoulder. The triceps relaxes to allow this movement to happen. In this action, the biceps is the prime mover or **agonist**, while the triceps is the secondary mover or **antagonist**.

Muscles are attached to bones at either side of joints by **tendons**. These are very strong cords of connective tissue that are embedded into the surface of the bone.

Key terms

Agonist The prime mover – muscle that causes movement.

Antagonist Muscle that relaxes to allow the agonist to contract.

Tendons Attach muscles to bones.

Muscle contraction for movement

There are two types of muscle contraction, isotonic and isometric:

Isotonic contractions occur when the muscle changes length as it contracts and causes movement of a body part. There are two types of isotonic contraction:

Concentric contractions are those where the muscle shortens as it contracts. An example is bending the elbow from straight to fully flexed, caused by a concentric contraction of the biceps muscle. Concentric contractions are the most common type of muscle contraction and occur frequently in sporting activities.

Eccentric contractions are the opposite of concentric and occur when the muscle lengthens as it contracts. This is less common than a concentric contraction and usually involves the control or slowing down of a movement started by the eccentric muscle's agonist.

In the downward phase of a press-up, the triceps contracts eccentrically to slow the movement down. Similarly, in a squat, the quadriceps contracts eccentrically to lower the body slowly towards the ground.

During **isometric** contractions, the muscle remains the same length. While performing a handstand, many of the body's muscles are contracting, but there is no movement as the balance is being held.

✔ Check your understanding

1. What is the difference between an isotonic and an isometric muscle contraction?
2. What is the difference between a concentric and an eccentric muscle contraction?
3. Give three examples of an isometric muscle contraction in three different physical activities.

Answers are on page 174.

Planes and axes

To better understand movements, scientists use specific terms to describe the way different parts of the body are moving.

Movements are described as taking place in one of three planes. At a simple level, these three planes are:

- **Sagittal** – forward or backward movements
- **Frontal** – side to side movements
- **Transverse** – rotational or turning movements.

To picture these three planes, imagine slicing through the body:

- First, through the centre, dividing the body into left and right parts – this is the **sagittal plane**.
- Next, through the body from the left side to the right, separating the front and back halves to create the **frontal plane** (front side and back side).
- Finally, cutting straight through the hips to divide the top of the body from the bottom; this creates the **transverse plane**.

Key terms

Isotonic Muscle action where the muscle changes length – causes movement.

Isometric Muscle action where the muscle stays the same length – used in balances.

Concentric Isotonic contraction where the muscle shortens.

Eccentric Isotonic contraction where the muscle lengthens – used to control downward movements.

Study hint

Remember, the first answer you give for movement questions will be the one that is marked.

Rapid recall

All **downward** movements, such as during push-ups and squats, involve **eccentric** contractions where the agonist controls the descent.

Study hint

You must make it clear which part of a question you are answering. This is especially important if there is an 'and' in the question.

An axis is a straight line that an object rotates or turns around. Movements of a joint are simply rotations. Bending the arm at the elbow actually involves rotating the forearm around the elbow joint. Movements at a joint take place in a certain plane about a certain axis. There are three axes of rotation:

- Transverse axis
- Sagittal axis
- Longitudinal axis.

The **transverse axis** passes horizontally through the body from left to right. Movements in a sagittal plane (forwards and backwards) take place around a transverse axis.

The **sagittal axis** passes horizontally through the body from back to front. Movements in a frontal plane (side to side) take place around a sagittal axis.

The **longitudinal axis** passes vertically from the top of the body to the feet. Movements in a transverse plane (rotations) take place around a longitudinal axis.

Key terms

Sagittal plane and transverse axis Plane and axis for forwards and backwards movements – direction for extension and flexion.

Frontal plane and sagittal axis Plane and axis for side to side movements – direction for abduction and adduction.

Transverse plane and longitudinal axis Plane and axis for rotating movements – direction for rotations and spins.

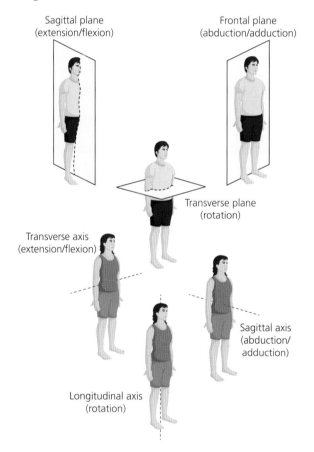

▲ Image showing planes and axes.

It is normal to describe a movement as taking place in the particular plane that the movement is dominated by. An example of this would be describing walking as taking place in a sagittal plane.

▼ Examples of dominant planes, actions and axes in movements.

PLANE	MOTION	AXIS	EXAMPLE
Sagittal	Flexion/extension	Transverse	Walking, running, squats, biceps curl, leg extensions, front somersault
Frontal	Abduction/adduction	Sagittal	Star jump, cartwheel, side-bending
Transverse	Rotations	Longitudinal	Discus and hammer throws, 360° twist, ice-skating spin

Activity

Stand in the corner of a room with your back against one wall. The walls and the ceiling (or floor) are in the same position as the planes of the body. The wall behind you that follows the line of your shoulders is the same as the frontal plane. The wall to the side of you that is going straight ahead is in the sagittal plane and the floor (or ceiling) shows the transverse plane.

Activity

Repeat the idea of standing in a corner (see opposite), but this time think about holding a bicycle wheel. If you position the wheel so the tyre follows the line of the walls (sagittal and frontal planes), then the spindle/axle in the wheel shows the axis of rotation of the plane (transverse and sagittal). The same process works for the transverse plane shown by the floor or ceiling and the longitudinal axis shown by the axle.

✔ Check your understanding

1 When a performer runs during a 100 m sprint, through which plane and in what axis do their legs move?
2 When a hammer thrower performs their throw, in which plane and in what axis does their movement occur?
3 As part of a training programme a performer completes star jumps. In which plane and in what axis are these movements performed?

Answers are on page 174.

Movement analysis

Movements in the sagittal plane about the transverse axis

When movements occur in the sagittal plane and around a transverse axis, the movements are called flexion and extension.

At the shoulder, flexion involves moving the whole arm forwards. The main agonist causing flexion at the shoulder is the **deltoid**.

Extension at the shoulder involves moving the whole arm backwards. The main agonist causing extension at the shoulder is the **latissimus dorsi**.

Shoulder flexion occurs during backstroke swimming and when serving at badminton. The action of the upper arm during sprinting also involves flexion (and extension) at the shoulder.

Activity

One of the best ways of finding out which is the main agonist is to prevent the movement happening and feel which muscle is working.

Key terms

Deltoid Muscle causing flexion at the shoulder.

Latissimus dorsi Muscle causing extension at the shoulder.

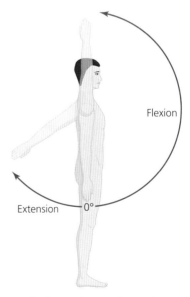

▲ Flexion and extension at the shoulder.

▲ Flexion occurring at the shoulder during the badminton serving action.

Flexion

Extension

▲ Flexion and extension at the elbow.

Key terms

Biceps Muscle causing flexion at the elbow.

Triceps Muscle causing extension at the elbow.

Hamstrings Group of muscles causing flexion at the knee.

Quadriceps Group of muscles causing extension at the knee.

Flexion

of knee joint

Extension

▲ Flexion and extension at the knee.

Flexion also occurs at the elbow. This involves the elbow bending and the hand moving towards the shoulder. The main agonist producing flexion at the elbow is the **biceps**.

Extension at the elbow is where the arm straightens. The main agonist causing extension at the elbow is the **triceps**.

These movements occur when performing a throw-in during football or rugby, and when shooting in basketball or netball.

Rapid recall

The weight-training exercise is called a biceps curl because during the 'curl' or upward movement, the biceps is the agonist.

✓ Check your understanding

1 What is the main agonist causing extension at the shoulder?
2 Name the movement caused by the triceps at the elbow.
3 What type of muscle contraction is occurring during the downward phase of a push-up? Name the main agonist.

Answers are on page 174.

Flexion at the knee is where the joint bends and the heel moves towards the back of the upper leg. The main agonist causing this movement is the **hamstrings** group of muscles.

Extension at the knee is where the knee straightens. The main agonist causing this movement is the **quadriceps** group of muscles.

Flexion and extension at the knee occurs when running, jumping and kicking. During the upward and downward phases of a squat there is flexion and extension at the knee.

Rapid recall

Flexion occurs when the angle between the bones in a joint **decreases**; extension is when the angle **increases**.

Flexion and extension also occurs at the hip joint. Flexion at the hip occurs when the straight leg moves forwards from a standing position. Flexion at the hip also occurs when you raise the leg off the floor when lying on your back. The main agonist during flexion at the hip is a group of muscles called the **hip flexors**.

Extension occurs when the leg is lowered down to the ground from a lying position and when that straight leg is returned to the standing position. The muscles causing extension at the hip, the agonists, are the **gluteals**.

Note that hip flexion and extension still occur when the knee is bent (flexed) as long as the upper leg (femur) is moving towards the upper body (flexion) or away from the upper body (extension).

Movements at the ankle are not called flexion or extension – rather they are known as **plantar flexion** and **dorsiflexion**, even though they occur in the sagittal plane and around a transverse axis.

Dorsiflexion is the equivalent to flexion and involves the **tibialis anterior** muscles contracting and pulling the toes up towards the shin bone.

Plantar flexion is the equivalent to extension and involves the **gastrocnemius** muscle contracting to push the foot out straight.

Plantar flexion occurs when running and jumping. Plantar flexion and dorsiflexion occur when kicking and when performing squats.

Rapid recall

Plantar flexion is when you point your toes.

✅ Check your understanding

1 Distinguish between plantar flexion and dorsiflexion.
2 Describe the movements occurring at the knee and name the agonist involved in the action of kicking a ball.
3 What type of muscle contraction is occurring during the downward phase of a squat? Name the main agonist.

Answers are on page 174.

Movements in the frontal plane about a sagittal axis

Abduction at the shoulder is the action of moving the arms away from the body in a frontal plane and around a sagittal axis.

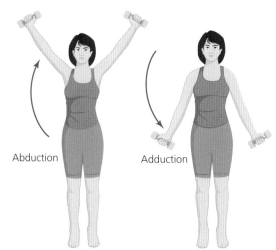

▲ Abduction and adduction at the shoulder.

In abduction, the main agonist is the **deltoid** muscle. The downward movement is called adduction and there are two main agonists, the **latissimus dorsi** and the pectorals. Abduction and adduction occur in a frontal plane around a sagittal axis.

Abduction and adduction occur during swimming the butterfly stroke. Throwing the arms forward above the water is abduction; dragging the arms back through the water is adduction.

Key terms

Hip flexors Main agonists at the hip during hip flexion.

Gluteals Main agonists at the hip during hip extension.

Tibialis anterior Muscle causing dorsiflexion at the ankle.

Gastrocnemius Muscle causing plantar flexion at the ankle.

▲ Hip flexion and extension.

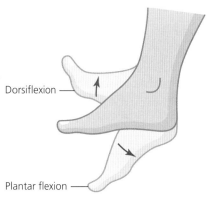

▲ Plantar flexion and dorsiflexion.

Key terms

Deltoid Muscle causing abduction at the shoulder.

Latissimus dorsi Muscle causing adduction at the shoulder.

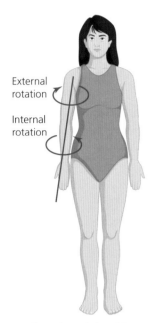

External rotation

Internal rotation

▲ Rotation of shoulder.

Key term

Rotator cuff Group of muscles causing rotation at the shoulder.

> ✔ **Check your understanding**
>
> 1 What two movements can the deltoids cause at the shoulder?
> 2 Which plane and what axis are involved in abduction and adduction?
> 3 What movement does the rotator cuff group of muscles cause?
>
> Answers are on page 174.

Movements in the transverse plane about the longitudinal axis

Turning the hand and forearm over while keeping the elbow straight (extended) means that the shoulder is rotating.

The shoulder can be rotated by turning the arm towards the body (internal rotation) or away from the body (external rotation). The main agonists causing internal and external rotation are the **rotator cuff** muscles. Rotation at the shoulder occurs when bowling in cricket.

▲ Rotation at shoulder during the cricket bowling action.

> **Rapid recall**
>
> **Rotation** at the shoulder is caused by the **rotator** cuff muscles.

Analysis of selected movements

Push-ups

▲ The movements during a push-up.

There are two parts to a push-up: the upward movement from B to A (pushing-up phase) and the downward movement from A to B (lowering-down phase).

In the pushing-up phase, there is movement at the elbow. The elbow straightens. This is extension, and the main agonist during this movement is the triceps. During this movement there is a concentric contraction of the triceps muscle.

In the lowering-down phase, the elbow bends. This is **flexion**. This movement has to be controlled eccentrically by the triceps muscle.

Football throw-in

A   B

▲ The movements during a throw-in.

A football (or rugby) throw-in starts with the ball behind the head (position A) and finishes with the ball leaving the hands (position B). During this movement there is extension at the elbow. This is brought about by a concentric contraction of the triceps muscle.

> ✔ **Check your understanding**
>
> 1 Complete the following table to describe the type of contraction, main agonist and joint actions occurring at the elbow during a push-up movement.
>
> | | Type of contraction | Main agonist | Joint action |
> |---|---|---|---|
> | Upward phase | | | |
> | Downward phase | | | |
>
> Answers are on page 175.

Running

A   B

▲ Leg action during running.

During running, movements occur at the hip, knee and ankle joints. The movements involved in running take place in a sagittal plane and around a transverse axis.

During running, there is a short period of time when the performer's foot is in contact with the ground and the performer pushes off the floor. This is the **drive phase** of running.

During this phase the knee straightens. This is extension. This movement is brought about by a concentric contraction of the quadriceps muscle.

Also during this phase, the hip extends. This is brought about by a concentric contraction of the gluteal muscles.

At the same time, the performer pushes off the ground using their ankle joint. This involves plantar flexion. This is caused by a concentric contraction of the gastrocnemius muscle.

After the drive phase, there is the **recovery phase** when the leg is brought forward to start another stride.

During the recovery phase the knee joint bends. This is flexion, which is caused by a concentric contraction of the hamstrings muscle.

During this phase the hip flexes because of a concentric contraction of the hip flexor muscles.

Also during recovery, the ankle adjusts. There is dorsiflexion, caused by a concentric contraction of the tibialis anterior muscle.

Kicking

Kicking is very similar to the drive phase of running. At the knee, the movement is from a bent knee to a straight knee. This is extension. Extension at the knee is caused by a concentric contraction of the quadriceps muscle.

At the hip there is flexion caused by a concentric contraction of the hip flexors.

During the kicking action the ankle remains plantar flexed throughout the movement. This is caused by an isometric contraction of the gastrocnemius muscle.

▲ Kicking action.

> **✔ Check your understanding**
>
> 1 Complete the following table to describe the type of contraction, main agonist and joint actions occurring at the hip, knee and ankle during the kicking action.
>
> | | Type of contraction | Main agonist | Joint action |
> |---|---|---|---|
> | Hip | | | |
> | Knee | | | |
> | Ankle | | | |
>
> 2 Describe the joint action and name the type of contraction that occurs at the ankle during kicking.
> 3 Describe the movements occurring at the knee and ankle during the recovery phase of running.
>
> Answers are on page 175.

Standing vertical jump

The standing vertical jump starts with the performer in a crouched position. During the movement there is extension at the hip due to a concentric contraction of the gluteal muscles. There is also extension at the knee caused by a concentric contraction of the quadriceps muscle. There is also plantar flexion at the ankle, caused by a concentric contraction of the gastrocnemius muscle.

Squats

There are two distinct movements in a squat. There is the upward phase from B to A, and there is the downward phase from A to B.

During the upward phase, the hip extends as the gluteals contract concentrically. During the downward phase, flexion occurs at the hip. This is controlled by an eccentric contraction of the gluteal muscles.

During the upward phase, the knee straightens. This is extension and is caused by a concentric contraction of the quadriceps muscle.

During the downward phase, the action taking place at the knee is flexion. This is caused by an eccentric contraction of the quadriceps muscle as it controls the descent.

A small amount of movement also occurs at the ankle during the upward phase of the squat. This is plantar flexion caused by a concentric contraction of the gastrocnemius muscle.

During the downward phase, the movement at the ankle is dorsiflexion. This is controlled by an eccentric contraction of the gastrocnemius muscle.

▲ Standing vertical jump.

▲ Squats.

Shoulder action during cricket bowling

During the bowling action of a cricketer there are two movements to note. There is rotation at the shoulder. This is caused by the action of the rotator cuff muscles. Rotation occurs in a transverse plane and around a longitudinal axis.

There is also extension at the shoulder, mainly caused by the action of the deltoids muscle.

✔ Check your understanding

1 Name the plane and axis involved in rotation at the shoulder.
2 Complete the following table to describe the type of contraction, main agonist and joint actions occurring at the knee during a squat.

	Type of contraction	Main agonist	Joint action
Upward phase			
Downward phase			

3 Complete the following table to describe the type of contraction, main agonist and joint actions occurring at the ankle during a squat.

	Type of contraction	Main agonist	Joint action
Upward phase			
Downward phase			

Answers are on page 175.

PRACTICE QUESTIONS

1. The diagram shows a sprinter leaving the starting blocks.

| A | B | C |

What type of muscle contraction is occurring in this muscle in diagram **A**, and during sequence **B–C**? (2 marks)

2. The image shows the gymnast in a press-up position.

a) Name the main *agonist* and *antagonist* at the elbow joint as the gymnast moves from position **A** (up position) to position **B** (down position). (2 marks)

b) Name the types of muscle contraction that occur at:
  (i) position **A** (up position) while the performer is stationary and;
  (ii) as the performer moves from position **A** (up position) to position **B** (down position). (2 marks)

c) Using the image, identify through what plane and about which axis the elbow action takes place. (2 marks)

3. The image shows phases of a tennis stroke.

A   B   C   D

a) What joint actions are taking place at:
  (i) the right **shoulder** during the sequence B–C?
  (ii) the right **elbow** during the sequence C–D? (2 marks)

b) In the same sequence C–D, name the *agonist* causing the movements at the elbow joint, and name the type of muscle contraction involved. (2 marks)

c) In which *plane* and around what *axis* does the shoulder movement C–D take place? (2 marks)

Answers are on pages 175.

Summary

- There are three classes of levers in the body
- Different lever systems have different advantages
- Different joints permit different types of movement
- These movements occur in various planes and axes
- The movements are caused by various muscles

Chapter objectives

- The relationship between health and fitness
- The components of fitness
- How to evaluate the need for components of fitness in specific physical activities and sport
- Reasons for carrying out fitness tests
- The protocol and procedures which should be followed when carrying out fitness tests
- The limitations of carrying out fitness tests
- How qualitative and quantitative data can be gained and used when fitness testing
- The principles of training and overload and how they can be applied to training programmes
- The varying training types and the advantages and disadvantages of using them
- How training can be structured into seasons
- The reasons for warming up and cooling down

The relationship between health and fitness

The definitions of health and fitness are also covered in Chapter 6 on health, fitness and well-being. This chapter deals with the relationship between health and fitness whereas Chapter 6 looks in detail at the components of health and well-being.

Definitions of health and fitness

Health (as per the World Health Organization's definition: 1948) – 'A state of complete physical, mental and social well-being and not merely the absence of disease or infirmity.'

Be aware that 'ill health' refers to being in a state of poor physical, mental and/or social well-being.

Fitness – The ability to meet/cope with the demands of the environment.

Key terms

Health A state of complete physical, mental and social well-being and not merely the absence of disease or infirmity.

Fitness The ability to meet/cope with the demands of the environment.

▲ To be 'healthy' is to be physically, mentally and socially well.

Looking at these terms, it is important to fully appreciate the relationship between health and fitness. It perhaps seems obvious that if you are in a good state of fitness, you are more likely to be healthy – certainly physically, but also mentally. Developing a good fitness level allows you to cope better with the demands of your daily life and environment and can help to lessen the potential to be affected by illness and disease.

However, it is important to realise that irrespective of how fit you are, there is always the potential to become unwell, i.e. suffer poor health.

The relationship between health and fitness can be summarised in the following points:

- Ill health can negatively affect fitness as the individual may be too unwell to train – thus lowering their fitness.
- Ill health may not affect fitness if the person is still well enough to train.
- Increases in fitness can positively affect health and well-being, e.g. you may be less likely to contract certain illnesses and diseases, you may feel content/happy within yourself and you may have enhanced your social well-being through taking part in activities.
- However, increased fitness cannot prevent you from contracting some illnesses and diseases and subsequently your health may suffer.

N.B. Over training (training too much) can in fact lower your immune system and make you more susceptible to illness and disease!

PRACTICE QUESTION

Which **one** of the following is correct?

A person who trains regularly and has a high level of fitness will:

- definitely not catch any illness or disease ☐
- be less likely to catch some illnesses or diseases ☐
- definitely have good mental health and well-being ☐
- definitely not have any friends or social well-being. ☐ (1 mark)

Answer is on page 177.

The components of fitness, benefits for sport and how fitness is measured and improved

There are numerous components of fitness; however, for GCSE Physical Education you are required to know, define and understand the following:

Study hint

It is a common mistake to suggest that increased fitness definitely improves health.

 Check your understanding

Can you define health and fitness and suggest some elements of the relationship between the two?

Answers are on page 176.

▲ Argentinian footballer Jonas Gutierrez had to stop playing football for some time to receive treatment for cancer.

Activity

Class debate

'Does an increase in a person's fitness definitely mean that they will be healthier'?

▲ Footballers often change direction quickly (at speed) to outwit opponents.

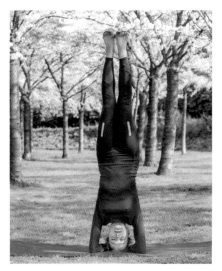

▲ Maintaining the centre of mass over the base of support in a headstand.

Key terms

Agility The ability to move and change direction quickly (at speed) whilst maintaining control.

Balance Maintaining the centre of mass over the base of support.

Check your understanding

Can you provide reasons/justifications why agility is needed by different sports performers?

Answers are on page 176.

For each of these components of fitness it is important that you can link them to specific sports and skills, justifying why they are needed.

Agility

Agility is simply defined as 'the ability to move and change direction quickly (at speed) whilst maintaining control'. In summary, agility involves:

- changing direction quickly or at speed
- maintaining control.

Agility combines speed, co-ordination, reaction time and strength and is applicable to most sporting scenarios. However, events like the 100 metres do not require agility as the runner does not change direction. As with all of the components of fitness, you may need to justify why agility is actually needed. It is not enough to simply state 'you need agility to change direction quickly'. Thus a footballer who does need to change direction quickly does so to outwit another player, or to manoeuvre themselves into a suitable position to pass or shoot. Similarly, it is true that a volleyball player may need to change direction quickly so that they can react to the opposing team's use of the ball.

Activity

Can you complete the table in order to justify why agility is required in the following sporting examples?

EXAMPLE SPORTING SCENARIO	JUSTIFICATION
Rugby player	Needs to change direction to avoid a tackler or to perform a side-step
Hockey player	
Badminton player	
Dancer	

Answers are on page 181.

Balance

Balance is defined as 'the maintenance of the centre of mass over the base of support'.

It is important to realise that there are in fact two different types of balance:

- Static balance (balancing whilst still), and
- Dynamic balance (maintaining balance whilst moving).

An example of static balance is when performing a headstand, which is in a held position. An example of dynamic balance is simply when walking, or, more complexly, when a snowboarder aims not to fall over when making his or her downhill descent.

Balance is an essential ingredient in all sports. You get no plaudits in any sport for falling over!

Activity

Gymnastics is an activity where there are many examples of when balance is particularly important. Can you complete the table to justify why balance is needed?

GYMNASTIC EXAMPLE	TYPE OF BALANCE	JUSTIFICATION
Handstand		Position of handstand has to be held whilst maintaining control, e.g. no wobbles
Headstand	Static	
Cartwheel along a beam		Moving along the beam without falling off Maintain control during the jump/rotation/movement
Tumble	Dynamic	

Answers are on page 181.

Cardio-vascular endurance

Cardio-vascular endurance can also be called 'aerobic power'. It is linked closely to stamina, which is being able to exercise whilst delaying the onset of fatigue. The definition of cardio-vascular endurance is 'the ability of the heart and lungs to supply oxygen to the working muscles'.

Cardio-vascular endurance is particularly important for sports performers who:

- perform long, enduring events
- perform using the aerobic energy system (using oxygen).

Thus you can say that cardio-vascular endurance is important for long distance runners, team sports performers, endurance cyclists and rowers (see Chapter 1c).

Marathon runners

Marathon runners run for 26 miles 385 yards. It is a long, gruelling event that requires the athlete to make best use of their aerobic energy system. Their ability to use oxygen is a key ingredient in whether they succeed or not.

Example scenario:

- Athlete A: A marathon runner with good cardio-vascular endurance will be good at supplying oxygen to the working muscles.
- Athlete B: A marathon runner with poor cardio-vascular endurance will be poor at supplying oxygen to the working muscles.
- Summary: Athlete B will tire quickly and will not be able to run as fast as athlete A.

Javelin thrower

As an event, javelin lasts only a few seconds and is explosive/powerful. It does not matter if a javelin thrower can supply oxygen to the working muscles for a long period of time. Thus, cardio-vascular endurance is not required by a javelin thrower.

Check your understanding

Define balance. Name two different types of balance. Explain why balance is needed for certain sporting activities.

Answers are on page 176.

Key term

Cardio-vascular endurance The ability of the heart and lungs to supply oxygen to the working muscles.

Activity

In small groups discuss whether cardio-vascular endurance is needed by a basketball player?

Answers are on page 181.

Study hint

It is important that you can justify why/why not cardio-vascular endurance is needed by sports performers.

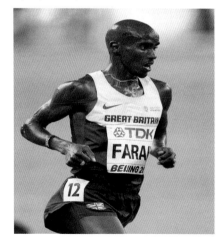

▲ Distance runners require a good level of cardio-vascular endurance.

✔ Check your understanding

Define cardio-vascular endurance and suggest reasons why it is needed by performers in different sports.

Answers are on page 176.

Key term

Co-ordination The ability to use different (two or more) parts of the body together smoothly and efficiently.

PRACTICE QUESTION

10,000 m in athletics is completed by running round a 400 m track 25 times. Would this require cardio-vascular endurance? Justify your answer. **(2 marks)**

Answer is on page 177.

Key term

Flexibility The range of movement possible at a joint.

Study hint

If two or more body parts are being used, co-ordination is needed.

✔ Check your understanding

Define co-ordination and suggest reasons why it is needed by performers in different sports.

Answers are on page 176.

Co-ordination

Co-ordination is defined as 'the ability to use different (two or more) parts of the body together smoothly and efficiently'.

In simple terms, it involves effective interaction of body parts, e.g. the eyes and the hands (hand-eye co-ordination). The nervous signals from the brain are timed to ensure effective use of appropriate muscles, e.g. signals are sent to the shoulders, arms and hands to catch a ball.

Some examples of co-ordination being used in sport include:

- hitting a cricket ball with a bat (hand-eye co-ordination)
- kicking a football (foot-eye co-ordination)
- arms and legs when dribbling a basketball (arms-legs co-ordination).

Flexibility

Flexibility is defined as 'the range of movement possible at a joint'. The joints of the body have maximum ranges of movement which differ in relation to the type of joint being used, e.g. a ball and socket joint allows a wider range of movement than a hinge joint (see joints, Chapter 1a). Developing good flexibility is beneficial as it can prevent individuals from sustaining an injury if their body moves out of the normal range of movement.

▲ A gymnast showing incredible flexibility.

Flexibility is required to different extents by different sports people. A gymnast usually needs a good range of movement in many of their joints to create the shapes and moves required in a floor routine, e.g. performing the splits.

Muscular endurance (similar to dynamic strength)

Muscular endurance is the ability of a muscle or muscle group to undergo repeated contractions, avoiding fatigue. The repeated contractions cause a limb to carry out repeated movement. The ability of a muscle/muscle group to move a limb repeatedly is needed for activities such as middle-distance running, rowing or swimming. Swimming strokes are repeated, forceful movements that need to be sustained.

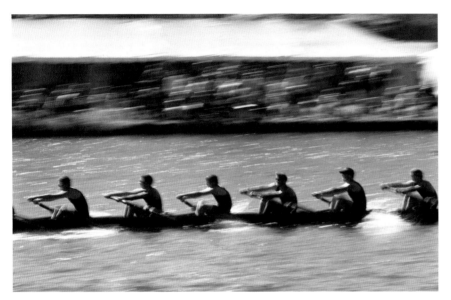

▲ Rowers perform repeated contractions causing their limbs to carry out the strokes required. This involves muscular endurance.

Power/explosive strength (anaerobic power)

Power, also known as explosive strength or anaerobic power is the product of strength and speed, i.e. strength x speed.

The creation of 'power' is useful in many sporting skills, for example:

- to generate power whilst kicking a football – kicking with strength, moving the leg at speed
- to smash/spike a volleyball with power – hitting with strength, moving the arm at speed
- to release a discus with power – releasing with strength, moving the arm at speed
- to perform a punch with power in boxing – punching with strength, moving the arm at speed.

In all of these examples, strength is exerted at speed to create the power.

Check your understanding

Define flexibility and suggest reasons why it is needed by performers in different sports.

Answers are on page 176.

Key term

Muscular endurance Ability of a muscle or muscle group to undergo repeated contractions avoiding fatigue.

Check your understanding

Define muscular endurance and suggest reasons why it is needed by performers in different sports.

Answers are on page 176.

Rapid recall

You can simply remember that power = strength x speed

Key term

Power The product of strength and speed, i.e. strength x speed.

✓ **Check your understanding**

Define power and suggest reasons why it is needed by performers in different sports?

Answers are on page 177.

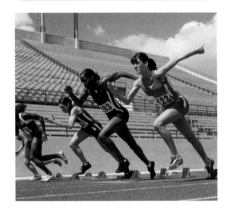

▲ The reaction time in sprinting is the time between the gun going off and the sprinter starting to initiate a response (starting to run).

Key term

Reaction time The time taken to initiate a response to a stimulus.

Activity

Can you calculate the following using distance divided by time?

If a sprinter runs 100 m in 10 seconds what is the average speed in metres per second?

Answer is on page 181.

Key term

Speed The maximum rate at which an individual is able to perform a movement or cover a distance in a period of time. Distance divided by time.

✓ **Check your understanding**

Define speed and suggest reasons why it is needed by performers in different sports?

Answers are on page 177.

▲ The point of release when throwing a discus requires strength to be exerted at speed (power).

Reaction time

Reaction time is the time taken to initiate a response to a stimulus – the time taken from the presentation of the stimulus to starting to initiate a response (e.g. gun sounding at start of 100 m to starting to move out of the blocks).

(Gun) ⟶ time to start reaction ⟶ (reaction starts/movement starts)

▲ Reaction time.

Speed

Speed is the maximum rate at which an individual is able to perform a movement or cover a distance in a period of time. It is also defined as 'putting the body parts through actions as quickly as possible'.

Speed can be calculated as 'distance divided by time'.

$$(speed = \frac{distance}{time})$$

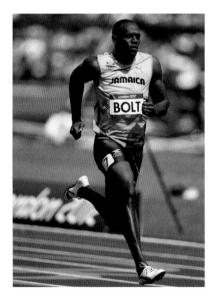

▲ Olympic sprinters show amazing speed, performing the 100 m in less than 10 seconds.

Strength

Strength is the ability to overcome a resistance. It relates to the force that can be produced by a muscle or group of muscles. This can be maximal, explosive, static or dynamic:

- Maximal The largest force possible in a single maximal contraction

- Dynamic (see Muscular endurance for similarity)

- Explosive (see Power)

- Static: The ability to hold a body part (limb) in a static position. Muscle length stays the same/maximum force that can be applied to an immovable object.

Maximal strength relates to the absolute maximum force that can be generated in one contraction. This is often tested using a one rep max test (see testing). It can be related to a single punch in boxing.

Dynamic strength relates more to repeated contractions (see muscular endurance).

Explosive strength is also known as power – the product of strength and speed. It can be expressed as strength × speed.

Static strength is applicable to scrummaging in rugby. When both teams push with the same force and the scrum is not moving, the muscles involved remain at the same length and force applied is maintained. (See isometric contraction Chapter 1a.)

Key term
Strength The ability to overcome a resistance.

▲ Strength demonstrated to lift a weight.

✔ Check your understanding

Can you define strength and suggest reasons why it is needed by performers in different sports?

Answers are on page 177.

Study hint

You may be required to define any of the components of fitness. You may also need to link physical activities and sports to the components of fitness, justifying why they may or may not be needed, e.g. a footballer needs agility because............

N.B. 'Justify' means to give a reason for your answer.

PRACTICE QUESTIONS

1. Is agility needed by a netball player? Justify your answer.　(2 marks)
2. Name a sport that requires participants to have good reaction time. Justify your answer.　(2 marks)
3. Which of these components of fitness is not required by a shot putter?
   - Power
   - Flexibility
   - Co-ordination
   - Muscular endurance

   (1 mark)
4. What is balance, and, using examples, why is it needed to play team games?　(4 marks)
5. What is speed and explain why a netball player may require good speed.　(2 marks)
6. In a sport like football, why might strength be needed?　(1 mark)
7. Using a sport of your choice, explain why cardio-vascular endurance is not needed.　(3 marks)

Answers are on page 177.

Reasons for carrying out fitness tests

It is often beneficial to test how proficient an individual is in a range of, or in specific components of, fitness. In simple terms, the main reasons for carrying out fitness tests can be summarised as:

- To identify strengths and/or weaknesses in a performance. Are there reasons for performing well or not so well? For example, perhaps your dribbling in a hockey match was poor because of a lack of speed?
- To inform your training requirements. As a result of initial tests, what components did you score poorly in and therefore may need to improve?
- To show a starting level of fitness. By testing at the start of a training programme, you can work out what level you are starting at. This links in well with the next point.
- To monitor improvement. Have the components of fitness you needed to improve actually improved over a period of time?
- To gauge the success of a training programme. If you have been training specific components of fitness you may test how well it has gone by undertaking fitness tests.
- To compare against norms of the group/national averages. You can compare results with your peers or, for an informed appraisal, some tests have national averages that you can compare your scores to.
- To motivate/set goals. Having knowledge that you will be doing fitness tests may well motivate an individual to try harder or to train in advance of the test so as to score well. It could also be that an individual is set a specific goal to achieve in the tests, thus providing them with motivation (drive).
- To provide variety in a training programme. Training programmes can be boring and lack variety. Carrying out tests either randomly or on a planned basis may well provide the variety required to keep individuals enthusiastic and motivated.

▲ Fitness testing can show you your strengths and weaknesses, what you need to improve and provide you with a starting point upon which to improve.

Fitness tests

The following fitness tests allow you to gain knowledge of:

- suitable tests for components of fitness
- what equipment is required
- what the protocol for each test is
- what the average is/national averages are for each test.

> **Activity**
>
> Why not try the tests out and compare your scores to the national averages/ratings provided? Please note that you should complete a thorough warm up (see page 76) prior to attempting any of the following tests.
>
> No test should be completed without the permission and/or supervision of a teacher/responsible adult.

Agility test – Illinois agility test

The test involves the following protocol:

- Equipment: 8 cones, a measuring tape and a stopwatch.
- The cones should be arranged in a 10 m x 5 m rectangle with 4 cones down the middle – see overleaf.

> **Rapid recall**
>
> The word **TEST** can be used to remember reasons for carrying out fitness tests.
>
> **T** Training programme – can inform you what needs to be trained
> **E** Evaluate strengths and weaknesses
> **S** Set goals – goals can be set, e.g. to achieve a specific score in a test
> **T** Tedium – to provide variety and avoid tedium/boredom in training

> **Activity**
>
> In small groups, discuss what fitness tests you have completed. Did anyone learn anything from the results? For example:
>
> - Did you score particularly well/poorly in a specific test?
> - Is there a component of fitness that you would benefit from training to improve?
> - Has anyone completed a test more than once in the last three years? Have they improved or got worse, and why?

Study hint
You may need to suggest the 'protocol' to carrying out fitness tests. This means: what do you actually do to carry out the test? Remember to use the correct units when describing a test, for example, one rep max in kilograms (kg).

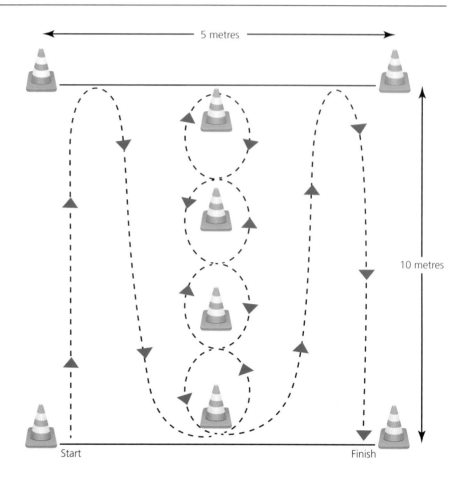

- Performer starts face down on the floor.
- The test involves running round the cones as fast as possible (it is a maximal test).
- It is timed in seconds, and
- It can be compared to the ratings below.

▼ Illinois agility test ratings.

RATING	MALES	FEMALES
Excellent	< 15.2	< 17.0
Above average	16.1–15.2	17.9–17.0
Average	18.1–16.2	21.7–18.0
Below average	18.3–19.2	23.0–21.8
Poor	> 19.3	> 23.0

Source: Davis, B. et al. (2000) *Physical Education and the Study of Sport*

Balance test – the 'stork balance' test

This test involves the following protocol:

- Equipment: a stopwatch is required.
- The individual starts balanced on two flat feet.
- Hands are placed on the hips.

- One leg is lifted so that the toes of the lifted leg touch the inside of the knee of the planted leg.
- The timekeeper tells the individual to raise the heel on the planted leg (and the stopwatch should start).
- The individual balances on one leg for as long as possible until they lose balance or have to move the toes attached to the inside of the knee.
- The time is recorded in minutes/seconds.
- The test can be repeated and scores are compared to the ratings below.

RATING	MALES	FEMALES
Excellent	< 50	< 30
Above average	41–50	23–30
Average	31–40	16–22
Below average	20–30	10–15
Poor	> 20	> 10

Source: Johnson and Nelson (1979) *Practical Measurements for Evaluation in Physical Education*

▲ Stork balance test.

Cardio-vascular endurance (aerobic power) test – multi-stage fitness test

The test involves the following protocol:

- Equipment: cones, tape measure (20 m or more), tape/CD with test, sheet to record score.
- It is run over a distance of 20 m, i.e. cones/line 20 m apart.
- It is progressive, i.e. it progressively gets harder.
- Individual runs 20 m in time with 'bleeps'.
- The time between bleeps gets shorter as the level increases.

20 metres

- The individual keeps running until they cannot keep up with the bleeps (maximal test) – N.B. If you do not get to the line in time, the individual is usually given one or two more attempts to 'catch up' with the timing of the bleeps.
- The score is recorded as a level and bleep, e.g. level 8 bleep 4, and compared to the ratings below. The score can provide a prediction of an individual's VO2 max (the maximum amount of oxygen that can be consumed per minute).

▼ Cardio-vascular endurance (aerobic power) test – multi-stage fitness test ratings.

MALES	VERY POOR	POOR	FAIR	AVERAGE	GOOD	VERY GOOD	EXCELLENT
12–13 yrs	< 3/3	3/4–5/1	5/2–6/4	6/5–7/5	7/6–8/8	8/9–10/9	> 10/9
14–15 yrs	< 4/7	4/7–6/1	6/2–7/4	7/5–8/9	8/10–9/8	9/9–12/2	> 12/2
16–17 yrs	< 5/1	5/1–6/8	6/9–8/2	8/3–9/9	9/10–11/3	11/4–13/7	> 13/7

FEMALES	VERY POOR	POOR	FAIR	AVERAGE	GOOD	VERY GOOD	EXCELLENT
12–13 yrs	< 2/6	2/6–3/5	3/6–5/1	5/2–6/1	6/2–7/4	7/5–9/3	> 9/3
14–15 yrs	< 3/3	3/4–5/2	5/3–6/4	6/5–7/5	7/6–8/7	8/8–10/7	> 10/7
16–17 yrs	< 4/2	4/2–5/6	5/7–7/1	7/2–8/4	8/5–9/7	9/8–11/10	> 11/11

Source: Adapted from Beep Test Ratings www.topendsports.com

Co-ordination test – wall toss test (Anderson ball catch test)

The test involves the following protocol:

- Equipment: a ball (usually a tennis ball), a flat wall, a stopwatch, an observer (timekeeper and scorer).
- The tennis ball starts in one hand.
- Both feet together, 2 m from the wall.
- Upon the command of 'go' the time starts – 30 seconds.
- The individual throws the ball against the wall and catches the ball with the opposite hand.
- This is repeated as many times as possible – counting 1, 2, 3, etc.
- Two attempts are allowed. If the ball is dropped the time continues.
- The score is compared to the ratings below.

RATING	SCORE (IN 30 SECONDS)
Excellent	> 35
Good	30–35
Average	20–29
Fair	15–19
Poor	< 15

▲ Anderson ball catch test.

Source: Adapted from Alternate Hand Wall Toss Test www.topendsports.com

Flexibility test – sit and reach test

The test involves the following protocol:

- Equipment: sit and reach box, slider (not available on all boxes).
- The individual adopts a sitting position on the floor with their legs straight.
- Shoes should be removed and feet should be flat against the sit and reach board.

- The slider (if available) should be set to 14 cm to be in line with the toes.
- The individual reaches forward and pushes the slider as far as possible.
- The score is recorded in centimetres and compared to the ratings below.

	MALES		FEMALES	
	CM	INCHES	CM	INCHES
Super	> +27	> +10.5	> +30	> +11.5
Excellent	+17 to +27	+6.5 to +10.5	+21 to +30	+8.0 to +11.5
Good	+6 to +16	+2.5 to +6.0	+11 to +20	+4.5 to +7.5
Average	0 to +5	0 to +2.0	+1 to +10	+0.5 to +4.0
Fair	−8 to −1	−3.0 to −0.5	−7 to 0	−2.5 to 0
Poor	−20 to −9	−7.5 to −3.5	−15 to −8	−6.0 to −3.0
Very poor	< −20	< −7.5	< −15	< −6.0

Source: Data supplied by Top End Sports www.topendsports.com

Muscular endurance test – abdominal curl conditioning test (sit-up bleep test)

The test for muscular endurance involves the following protocol:

- Equipment: partners for each participant, CD of test (NCF abdominal conditioning test), gym mat.
- Individual lies on the mat in sit-up position, partner supports ankles.
- The participant sits up on the bleep and down on the bleep (staying in time).
- The test is maximal – how many sit-ups can you do in time with the bleeps.
- It is also progressive – the bleeps get faster.
- The score is how many sit-ups you complete.
- Scores are compared to national averages (see below).

▲ Sit and reach test.

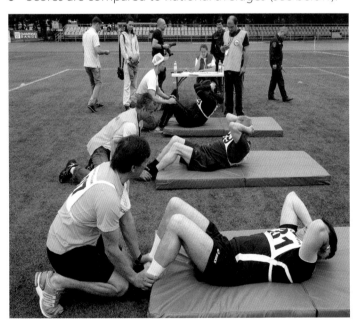

▲ Completing the test.

▼ Abdominal conditioning test ratings.

STAGE	TOTAL SIT-UPS	MALES	FEMALES
1	20	Poor	Poor
2	42	Poor	Fair
3	64	Fair	Fair
4	89	Fair	Good
5	116	Good	Good
6	146	Good	Very Good
7	180	Excellent	Excellent
8	217	Excellent	Excellent

Source: Adapted from NCF Abdominal Curl Conditioning Test www.topendsports.com

Power/explosive strength (anaerobic power) test – vertical jump test (sergeant jump test)

The test for leg power involves the following protocol:

- Equipment: wall ruler, usually 2 m.
- Feet flat, stand and push the wall ruler with the fingertips as high as possible.
- This provides the individual's 'zero point'.
- Apply chalk (or something to make a mark) to the finger tips.
- From a standing position, the individual jumps as high as possible marking the ruler with the chalk.
- The observer records the height jumped in cm.
- The score is compared to the ratings below.

▲ Performing the vertical jump test.

	MALES		FEMALES	
Rating	(inches)	(cm)	(inches)	(cm)
excellent	> 28	> 70	> 24	> 60
very good	24–28	61–70	20–24	51–60
above average	20–24	51–60	16–20	41–50
average	16–20	41–50	12–16	31–40
below average	12–16	31–40	8–12	21–30
poor	8–12	21–30	4–8	11–20
very poor	< 8	< 21	< 4	< 11

Source: http://www.topendsports.com/testing/tests/home-vertical-jump.htm

Reaction time test – ruler drop test

The test for reaction time involves the following protocol:

- Equipment: a metre ruler.
- One person holds the metre ruler at the zero point (vertically).
- The individual being tested places their thumb and index finger of their dominant hand around the ruler (not touching it) at 50 cm.
- Without warning the ruler is released.
- The individual being tested must react to the drop and catch the ruler as fast as they can (with their thumb and index finger).
- The score to be recorded is in cm – how far from 50 cm the individual caught the ruler.
- The individual may have three attempts.

▲ Performing the ruler drop test.

EXCELLENT	ABOVE AVERAGE	AVERAGE	BELOW AVERAGE	POOR
< 7.5 cm	7.5–9 cm	15.9–20.4 cm	20.4–28 cm	> 28 cm

Source: Norms, adapted from Davis (2000), for 16 to 19 year olds.

Maximal strength test – one rep max test

The test for one rep max involves the following protocol:

- Equipment: appropriate weights/resistance machine – usually a bar bell or bench press machine.
- Lift a weight once using the correct technique.
- If completed, attempt a heavier weight until the heaviest weight the individual can possibly lift once is discovered (one correctly completed repetition).
- If a weight cannot be lifted a lighter weight should be used to calculate the maximum weight that can be lifted.

▼ One rep max test ratings using bench press.

Take your 1 rep max weight for the bench press or leg press and **divide it** by your **body weight**. So, for example, if you were able to lift **300 lbs (136 kg)** on the leg press and you weigh **175 lbs (80 kg)**, that equates to a score of **1.7**.

▲ One rep max using a bench press.

Excellent	> 1.60
Good	1.30–1.60
Average	1.15–1.29
Below average	1.00–1.14
Poor	0.91–0.99
Very poor	< 0.90

Strength – handgrip dynamometer test

The test for strength involves the following protocol:

- Equipment: handgrip dynamometer.
- The dynamometer should be held in the individual's dominant hand. The arm should be at 90 degrees with the elbow against the body.

▲ Carrying out the handgrip dynamometer test.

- Grip may need to be adjusted to size.
- Squeeze with maximum effort and record score.
- Repeat three times and record best score.
- Compare to ratings as below.

▼ Grip strength ratings for males (in kg)

AGE	WEAK	NORMAL	STRONG
12–13	< 19.4	19.4–31.2	> 31.2
14–15	< 28.5	28.5–44.3	> 44.3
16–17	< 32.6	32.6–52.4	> 52.4
18–19	< 35.7	35.7–55.5	> 55.5

▼ Grip strength ratings for females (in kg).

AGE	WEAK	NORMAL	STRONG
12–13	< 14.6	14.6–24.4	> 24.4
14–15	< 15.5	15.5–27.3	> 27.3
16–17	< 17.2	17.2–29.0	> 29.0
18–19	< 19.2	19.2–31.0	> 31.0

Source: Camry Electronic Hand Dynamometer Instruction Manual

Speed test – 30 m speed test

The protocol for this test involves:

- Equipment: two cones 30 m apart, tape measure, stopwatch.
- Use a flying start.
- The individual is timed running 30 m as fast as they can.
- The score in seconds is compared to ratings.

▼ 30 m sprint test ratings.

	MALES	FEMALES
Excellent	< 4.0	< 4.5
Above average	4.2–4.0	4.6–4.5
Average	4.4–4.3	4.8–4.7
Below average	4.6–4.5	5.0–4.9
Poor	> 4.6	> 5.0

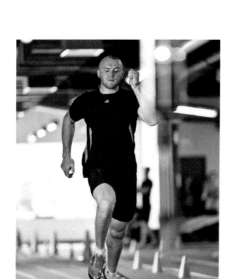

▲ Carrying out the 30 m sprint test.

Study hint

'Testing protocol' refers to how each test is carried out and organised. This includes equipment needed, rules to be followed, measurements and scoring and how comparisons and conclusions can be made, e.g. using ratings tables.

Limitations of fitness testing

Although there are numerous benefits from carrying out fitness tests it is fair to say that fitness tests also have their limitations. These can be summarised as:

- Tests are often not sport specific and can be too general. For example, the ruler drop test is not something that is carried out in any sport.
- They do not replicate movements of activities – very few sports involve direct running of 20 m up and down in a straight line like the multi-stage fitness test.
- They do not replicate competitive conditions required in sports – major sporting events are performed under extreme pressure. Many of the tests can be repeated/retried.
- Many of the tests have questionable reliability. As most tests are maximal, the individual must try their hardest in the test to gain an accurate score, thus motivation levels must be high. Also, as a partner sometimes measures your score – e.g. vertical jump test – it is possible that they will get the scoring wrong.
- The tests must be carried out with the correct procedures and protocols, otherwise scores will not be accurate or valid.

▲ The ruler drop test involves an action that is not sport specific.

> ✔ **Check your understanding**
>
> Name and describe how each test is carried out (protocol).
>
> Answers are on page 177.

Evaluating what tests are appropriate for different sporting performers

For GCSE Physical Education, you may be required to evaluate whether it is appropriate or relevant for certain sporting performers to carry out specific fitness tests, e.g. what tests are most appropriate for a tennis player? The table overleaf gives some examples of who each test is appropriate or less appropriate/inappropriate for.

Study hint

Validity means that the test actually tests what it states it will test. A valid test is one which is appropriate for the sport.

Reliability means that if the test is repeated, similar results can be gained.

TEST	REASONS WHY IT IS APPROPRIATE	REASONS WHY IT IS LESS OR INAPPROPRIATE
Illinois agility test	Tennis players need good agility to change direction at speed following the direction of the ball after it has been hit by their opponent	100m runners. They will not need to change direction, therefore do not need to be tested on this component
Stork balance test	Gymnasts may well hold balances still and therefore it is appropriate to work out how good their static balance is	Less appropriate for a squash player who is regularly on the move and seldom still
Multi-stage shuttle run test	Basketball players need good aerobic fitness and often run up and down the court	Golfers do not need to run up and down the fairway so it is less appropriate for them
Anderson wall toss test	Cricketers need good co-ordination and should be able to catch with both hands	Rowers need to co-ordinate their arms and legs but do not need to catch, so the test is less appropriate for them
Sit and reach test	Dancers need good flexibility in their legs to perform dances	Swimmers need flexibility but do not need hamstring flexibility as much as a dancer would, so the test is less appropriate for them
Sit-up bleep test	A goalkeeper in football may have to make regular saves involving movement of their upper and lower body so this test is appropriate for them	Marathon runners do need muscular endurance but the movement involved in the test does not mimic the movement of running so it is less appropriate for them
Vertical jump test	Basketball players need to jump using leg power	Kayaking requires no ability to apply leg power vertically
Ruler drop test	Cricketers may need to react quickly to an object (ball) using their hands	Snowboarders do need reaction time, but catching a ruler does not mimic any action they use, so it is less appropriate
One rep max test	Boxers may well need to exert maximal force in a punch	Middle-distance runners do not need to exert maximal force in a race
Handgrip dynamometer	Judo holds require maximal grip strength	Sprinters have no need to use grip strength
30 m speed test	Table tennis performers do need speed, but in their arms more than their legs	Discus throwers have no need to use speed

Study hint

Always try to work out what is needed in a sport before answering whether a test is or is not appropriate, e.g. shot putters do not need speed so the 30 m sprint test is not appropriate.

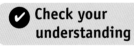

Check your understanding

Have a look at the fitness tests. Can you think of some sports in which participants would benefit from having that component of fitness tested? Share your answers with your classmates.

PRACTICE QUESTIONS

1. What equipment is needed for a multi-stage fitness test? (2 marks)
2. Suggest two benefits of using fitness tests. (2 marks)
3. Suggest two limitations of using fitness tests. (2 marks)
4. Would an Illinois agility test be appropriate for a netball player? Justify your answer. (3 marks)
5. Explain the protocol for carrying out a one rep max test. (3 marks)

Answers are on pages 178–179.

Qualitative and quantitative data

In relation to fitness testing, there are two terms that are often confused with each other – qualitative and quantitative. Qualitative data refers to opinions. There does not need to be a score or number as such, it could simply be a subjective appraisal – e.g. 'I did well in that test'. An individual who scores level 12, bleep 3 in the multi-stage fitness test may well look at the outcome qualitatively (It was a good score but I could have done better) rather than just as a quantitative measure (level 12, bleep 3). Quantitative data deals with quantities. The measurement is classified as a number or a score. An individual may well look at the ruler drop test as a quantitative figure only – e.g. 'I scored 15 cm'. (See Chapter 7 'Use of data'.)

Activity

If you are able to carry out any tests, compare your scores to national averages/ratings as shown. Complete the table by recording your quantitative score and complete a comment (opinion) about your score in the qualitative column, e.g. 'did really well'.

TEST	QUANTITATIVE SCORE	QUALITATIVE APPRAISAL
Illinois agility test		
Stork balance test		
Multi-stage shuttle run test		
Anderson wall toss test		
Sit and reach test		
Sit up bleep test		
Vertical jump test		
Ruler drop test		
One rep max test		
Handgrip dynamometer		
30 m speed test		

Key terms

Qualitative data A measure of opinions. More of a subjective than an objective appraisal relating to the quality of a performance rather than the quantity.

Quantitative data A measurement which has been quantified as a number, e.g. time in seconds, or goals scored. There is no opinion expressed (qualitative). It is a fact. It is often the case that quantitative scores in fitness tests can be compared to national averages/ratings.

Rapid recall

Remember:
Quantity – for quantitative. A quantity/number
Quality – for qualitative. An opinion – good/bad, etc.

PRACTICE QUESTION

What do you understand by the term 'quantitative' in relation to fitness testing?

(1 mark)

Answer is on page 179.

The principles of training and their application to personal exercise and training programmes

The principles of training

The principles of training refer to key principles which should always be considered when designing a training programme. They act as a guide and should be considered for all prolonged periods of training. The principles are often remembered as SPORT:

- **S**pecificity
- **P**rogressive **O**verload
- **R**eversibility
- **T**edium

Specificity

Specificity refers to the fact that training should be specific to the needs of an individual and the demands of the sport that they take part in. For instance, a sprinter would be likely to do more anaerobic, speed and power work as they are all important for that activity. Any training done should be specific to the muscles used and the energy demands of the activity. Cyclists, for example, will not lift heavy arm weights as their legs are the specific body part that do most of the work.

Key term

Progressive overload Working harder than normal whilst gradually and sensibly increasing the intensity of training.

Study hint

Overload does not mean to overburden the body as that would be classed as over-training. Overload is simply working harder than normal.

Rapid recall

When thinking about the principles of training, remember SPORT:

Specificity
Progressive
Overload
Reversibility
Tedium

✔ Check your understanding

Name and explain the principles of training and overload.

Answers are on page 177.

Progressive overload

Although overload and progression are often discussed separately, they can also be grouped together. Overload is simply 'working harder than normal'. By doing this the body will adapt and improve. However, progression refers to the fact that the overload should gradually be increased as the body adapts. The progressive overload on the body may mean gradually running further or lifting heavier weights. Training should sensibly overload the body as if it progresses too quickly, then an individual may suffer an injury.

Reversibility

Reversibility simply states that if an individual stops or decreases their training level, then fitness and performance are likely to drop. Muscle strength and cardio-vascular endurance can drop quite quickly if training is stopped altogether.

Tedium

Tedium refers to boredom. Training should be altered and varied to prevent an individual from suffering from this.

Key principles of overload

The principles of overload work on the idea that all training must overload the body's systems more than normal. Thus overload is working harder than normal. It is a fundamental concept of training – you must work harder than normal (overload) in order for the body to adapt and improve. There are four basic principles of overload that are particularly important for exercise at a low to medium intensity:

- Frequency
- Intensity
- Time
- Type.

These four guidelines (FITT) should be used when designing the amount of overload to be adopted within a training programme. The details of FITT include:

- **Frequency** – refers to how often someone trains. Normally training should take place three or more times a week. As fitness increases, the ability to train more often also becomes possible.

- **Intensity** – refers to how hard you train: how fast you run/how heavy the weight is that you are lifting, etc. As fitness increases, the intensity should be suitably increased.

- **Time** – refers to how long you train for. As fitness increases, the length of time spent training may well increase.

- **Type** – refers to the type of training used, e.g. continuous training. The training type must remain suitable to gain the specific fitness benefits that are required.

N.B. Further application of the principles of training are detailed in the section on training types.

Types of training

There are many different types of training. However, they each have their benefits and specific purposes that match specific sporting needs. As with all training, it is important that safety is maintained at all times (see safety when training below).

Circuit training

Circuit training is a flexible form of training in that it can be organised in a way to train many different components of fitness or to train a specific aspect, e.g. a circuit training programme could be organised to train various components of fitness required by rugby players (speed, power, strength, etc.).

Circuit training involves different exercises being organised in different areas (or stations). Each station can be completely different from the next. Completion of all of the stations is called 'a circuit'.

In order to organise circuit training, you need to consider many points:

- What is it that you hope to achieve, e.g. to improve one component of fitness or several different ones?
- How much space and equipment is available?
- How much work and time should each station have and how much time should be allocated to rest between stations? This is known as the 'work to rest ratio'.

It is perhaps most common that a circuit is designed to train different components of fitness and work on different muscles/body parts. The stations could well make use of shuttles, step-ups, sit-ups, squat jumps, burpees, squat jumps, etc.

An example for rugby would incorporate the principles of training in that:

- Specificity – circuits would focus on specific muscles used and aspects of fitness required in rugby
- Progressive overload – when the circuit is repeated, it should gradually be made harder
- Reversibility – the circuit should be repeated regularly to prevent loss of fitness
- Tedium – circuits should be varied to prevent boredom, e.g. shuttle runs, press-ups, sit-ups, vertical jumps/squats, quick rugby passes, etc. (all relevant to rugby)
- Frequency – may well be completed three times a week
- Intensity – depends on the fitness level but could start at 20 seconds of work/30 seconds of rest, with the circuit being completed three times. There may well be two minutes' rest between each circuit.
- Time – 30-minute session
- Type – circuit training

In the example above, it is key that the rugby player performs exercises that are appropriate and specific to rugby.

Study hint

Remember that for circuit training, altering the time/rest/content of the circuit will determine what the fitness aim of the circuit is.

PRACTICE QUESTIONS

1. What does the principle of frequency refer to?
   (1 mark)
2. What is meant by the term 'progressive overload'?
   (2 marks)
3. How should an individual apply the principle of specificity to a training programme? (2 marks)

Answers are on page 179.

Key term

Circuit training A series of exercises performed one after the other with a rest in between.

Study hint

Remember that fitness tests actually *test* a component of fitness. A one-off test does *not train* the component of fitness. Training types, e.g. continuous training, actually train a component of fitness.

Activity

Try to design a 6–10 station circuit for a sport of your choice. Make sure the stations involve muscles/movements and energy demands which are suitable for the sport. Try to suggest an appropriate work/rest ratio for you. A starting point may be to consider:

- 20 to 30 seconds' work on each exercise
- 30-second recovery between each exercise
- 3 sets with a 2–3 minute recovery between each set
- If you feel that your fitness level is higher you can try more work and less rest.

Advantages and disadvantages

Circuit training has many advantages:

- Exercises chosen can be simple to complex.
- The circuit can be manipulated to train different things, e.g. repeated contraction of a muscle/muscle group to train muscular endurance.
- It can be varied to suit fitness level/age, etc.
- It is easy to monitor and alter – progressive overload can be applied by altering the work/rest ratio.

Disadvantages of circuit training include:

- An appropriate amount of space is required.
- It may require specialist equipment, e.g. a medicine ball, benches.
- It is difficult to gauge an appropriate work/rest ratio at the start.

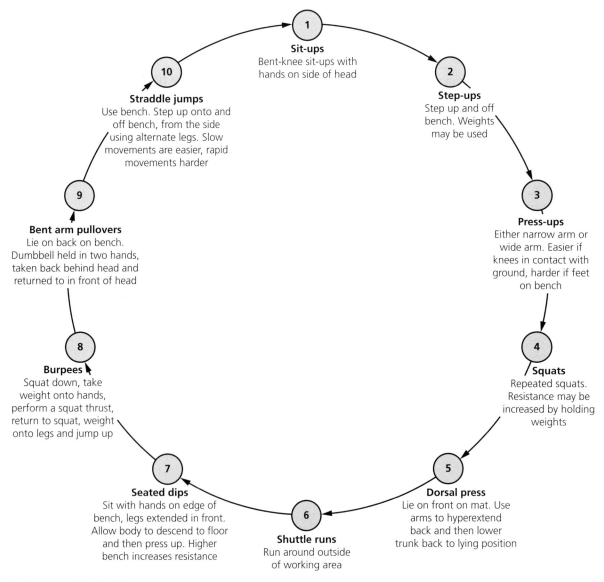

1
Sit-ups
Bent-knee sit-ups with hands on side of head

2
Step-ups
Step up and off bench. Weights may be used

3
Press-ups
Either narrow arm or wide arm. Easier if knees in contact with ground, harder if feet on bench

4
Squats
Repeated squats. Resistance may be increased by holding weights

5
Dorsal press
Lie on front on mat. Use arms to hyperextend back and then lower trunk back to lying position

6
Shuttle runs
Run around outside of working area

7
Seated dips
Sit with hands on edge of bench, legs extended in front. Allow body to descend to floor and then press up. Higher bench increases resistance

8
Burpees
Squat down, take weight onto hands, perform a squat thrust, return to squat, weight onto legs and jump up

9
Bent arm pullovers
Lie on back on bench. Dumbbell held in two hands, taken back behind head and returned to in front of head

10
Straddle jumps
Use bench. Step up onto and off bench, from the side using alternate legs. Slow movements are easier, rapid movements harder

▲ An example circuit.

Continuous training

Continuous training involves any activity that can be sustained without rest and repeated over and over – e.g. running, walking, rowing and swimming. Continuous training is used to improve cardio-vascular endurance and involves working at a constant rate or intensity. This is often referred to as '**steady state exercise**'.

Continuous training is intended to work the aerobic energy system. Therefore the difficulty or intensity should be hard enough to stress the body but with a suitable level of oxygen intake to ensure the exercise is 'aerobic'. To do this, it is most common to use your heart rate as a guide. This is known as working at your 'aerobic training zone'. In simple terms, you use your heart rate to tell you if you are working hard enough and prolonged continuous training makes your body more efficient at using oxygen.

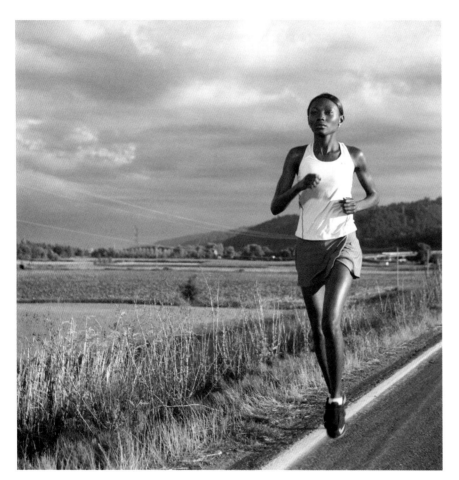

Continuous training:

1 involves using your heart rate as a guide

2 improves your cardio-vascular endurance

3 improves your ability to work without suffering fatigue, thus your stamina improves.

PRACTICE QUESTIONS

1. Name three things to consider when designing a circuit training session.
   (3 marks)

2. What do you understand by the term 'work/rest ratio'? (1 mark)

Answers are on page 179.

▲ A long steady state swim can be completed continuously.

Study hint

An untrained individual will continuously work quite slowly, whereas an elite athlete will be able to continuously work at a higher intensity.

Key terms

Continuous training Exercising for a sustained period of time without rest. It improves cardio-vascular fitness. Sometimes referred to as 'steady state' training.

Steady state exercise Working continuously at the same intensity.

N.B. Generally speaking, continuous training involves working without rests, for 20 minutes or more.

Application to the principles of training:

● The activity being completed should be *specific* to the sport – e.g. a marathon runner would tend not to swim in training as it is not specific to marathon running.

● The *frequency* for most continuous training programmes is a minimum of 3 times a week. However, a non-elite performer may only train once a week whereas an elite performer may train on most days of the week.

● Continuous training as a *training type* should only be used for activities which are long and enduring.

Advantages and disadvantages of continuous training

Continuous training has many advantages:

● It can be done with little or no equipment, e.g. simply go for a run.
● It improves aerobic fitness.
● Running can be done virtually anywhere.
● It is simple to do – keep doing the same movement over and over.

Disadvantages of continuous training:

● It can be boring/tedious.
● It can cause injury due to repetitive contractions.
● It can be time consuming.
● It does not always match the demands of the sport, e.g. in basketball the players do not run at one speed continuously.

Calculating the correct intensity for continuous training

As previously mentioned, calculating the aerobic training zone involves using your heart rate as a guide. This involves calculating your maximum heart rate in beats per minute and working at a percentage of this:

● Calculate maximum heart rate (220 minus age).
● Calculate aerobic training zone (60–80 per cent of maximal heart rate).

E.g. A 16 year old could calculate their aerobic training zone as follows:

● 220 – 16 (age) = 204
● 60–80 per cent of 204 = 122–163 beats per minute.

Thus when training continuously, the heart rate should remain between 122 and 163 beats per minute.

▲ Maximum heart rate is 220 minus age.

Activity

Can you calculate your aerobic training zone?

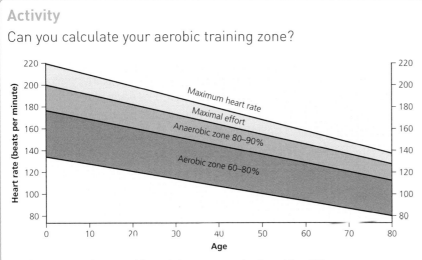

▲ Graph showing aerobic training zones calculated for different age groups.

As you can see in the image above, athletes may well decide to work at their anaerobic training zone of 80–90 per cent of maximal heart rate. This is useful for athletes whose activities are predominantly anaerobic, e.g. 400 m runners. An elite 400 m runner may well complete a circuit of the track in less than 50 seconds, meaning that the aerobic system has not been utilised. Thus, such an athlete needs to prepare their body in training to perform at this intensity, by training in their anaerobic zone.

Fartlek training

Like continuous training, fartlek training is generally used to improve cardio-vascular endurance. It is more varied than continuous training as the speed and intensity is varied. It is also known as 'speed play' and normally involves running.

Fartlek training involves:

- the speed being altered throughout – e.g. sprint, jog, walk, jog, sprint
- exercises being incorporated into the activity
- running on different terrains – e.g. running on the flat, on hills, etc.
- altering the intensity as this can allow the aerobic and anaerobic energy systems to be trained – e.g. the more sprints involved the more emphasis on the anaerobic system.

PRACTICE QUESTIONS

1. Using an example from a sport of your choice, why would a performer benefit from using continuous training? (2 marks)
2. How do you calculate an aerobic training zone? (1 mark)
3. Is continuous training appropriate for a 100 m sprinter? Justify your answer. (2 marks)
4. What is fartlek training? (2 marks)

Answers are on page179.

Interval training (high intensity interval training)

Interval training is the name given to any type of training that involves alternating periods of work with periods of rest. It usually involves periods of intense exercise (working hard) coupled with periods of rest or low intensity exercise. This form of interval training has become known as high intensity interval training or HIIT for short.

The intensity of interval training can be altered to suit the individual by altering the time working and the time resting.

HIIT basically means:

- short bursts of extreme effort with even shorter rest periods
- a 2:1 work ratio is often used, e.g. 30 seconds work, 15 seconds rest.

Beginners to interval training may well start with

- 2–3 HIIT sessions a week
- a 2:1 work ratio which may involve 20 seconds work/10 seconds recovery – with the aim to increase this to 30 seconds work/15 seconds recovery.

Key terms

Interval training Training method that incorporates periods of work followed by periods of rest, e.g. work, rest, work, rest.

HIIT High Intensity Interval Training: an exercise strategy alternating periods of short intense anaerobic exercise with less intense recovery periods.

Study hint

The higher the intensity of the work period, the shorter the duration, e.g. 90–100 per cent effort cannot be carried out for long.

An example HIIT session for a beginner is shown below:

- Perform a thorough warm up.
- Use: 30 seconds of work with 15 seconds of rest, working at 90 per cent of maximal effort.
- Perform press-ups, sit-ups, tricep dips, lunges, gluteal kicks or burpees.
- For example, 30 seconds of press-ups followed by 15 seconds of rest.
- Repeat three times.

Advantages and disadvantages of HIIT

Advantages of HIIT training:

- It burns body fat and calories quickly.
- It can be altered easily to suit the individual.
- It can be completed relatively quickly.
- It can improve the anaerobic and aerobic energy systems.

Disadvantages of HIIT training:

- Extreme work can lead to injury.
- High levels of motivation are needed to complete the work.
- It can lead to dizziness and feelings of nausea.

Use of interval training

Interval training can be altered to suit the needs of a performer. HIIT involves short high intensity periods of work that improve the anaerobic system. However, research has shown that HIIT also has benefits for the aerobic system. Thus it suits sports that make use of either energy system. If you're an elite performer athlete who needs energy systems to be trained for your sport, you can incorporate some sessions of sport-specific HIIT work. For example:

- sprints or high intensity dribbling for football players
- vertical jumps for volleyball and basketball players
- heavy bag interval work for boxers.

You can also vary the length of the intervals.

- High intensity anaerobic intervals can last anywhere from 10 to 60 seconds.
- Low intensity and more aerobic intervals can last several minutes.

✔ Check your understanding

Describe what HIIT is.
Answers are on page 177.

▲ Burpees are common exercises used in interval training.

As with all forms of training, it is important to remember the principles of training. Intervals should involve exercises and movements which are specific to the sport and intensity should match the intensity of the sport, e.g. high intensity sprints are fine if the sport requires some high intensity sprinting!

Activity

Why not try a basic HIIT training session working using a 2:1 work:rest ratio. Include 30 seconds (each) of press-ups, burpees, sit-ups and lunges with 15 seconds rest in between. Repeat the process three times.

Plyometric training

Plyometrics is a type of training that is used to increase power (strength x speed). It typically takes the form of bounding, hopping or jumping but can include medicine ball work, 'jump and clap' press-ups and box work. The aim of plyometrics is to use your body weight and gravity to stress the muscles involved. As an example, if we use box jumping:

1 The athlete jumps off the box.
2 As they land their quadriceps lengthen (eccentric contraction).

PRACTICE QUESTIONS

1. What do you understand by the term HIIT training?
   (1 mark)
2. Identify two benefits of using HIIT training.
   (2 marks)

Answers are on page 180.

3 This stores 'elastic energy' which can then be released through a further immediate jump.

4 The second jump (using the stored elastic energy) makes use of a stronger concentric contraction.

5 Thus the eccentric contraction has caused a stronger concentric contraction.

▲ Athlete using box jumping to increase their leg power.

Plyometrics can be used by any athlete who requires power. A basketball player or a triple jumper may well use plyometrics to increase their leg power for jumping. It is an excellent way to increase power but can result in injury due to the stress placed on the muscles and joints.

Static stretching

There are many different forms of stretching but perhaps the most common is that of static stretching. Static stretching is when a stretch is carried out and held (**isometric contraction**). It is an excellent way to increase flexibility – the range of movement at a joint.

Static stretches are often performed as part of a warm up or cool down but can be a form of training in themselves. They are used by performers who wish to improve their flexibility, e.g. gymnasts and dancers.

Static stretching involves:

- stretching to the limit
- holding the stretch (isometrically) for approximately 30 seconds
- avoiding over-stretching as injury can occur
- using the correct technique, e.g. avoid dangerous stretches such as straight-legged toe touches.

Advantages and disadvantages of static stretching

Advantages of static stretching:

- It increases flexibility (the range of movement at a joint).
- It can be done by virtually everyone.
- It is relatively safe.

Key terms

Static stretching Stretching to the limit and holding the stretch isometrically.

isometric contraction Muscular contraction when the muscle does not shorten or lengthen – it stays the same length.

▲ A static stretch being held.

Disadvantages of static stretching:

- It can be time consuming to stretch the whole body.
- Some muscles are easier to stretch than others.
- Over-stretching can cause injury.

Weight training

Weight training can be used by anyone and can involve the use of free weights, resistance machines or any object which can safely be lifted. The beauty of weight training is that it allows individuals to use and therefore train individual muscles/muscle groups and can be designed to suit an individual's needs. A tennis player may well design a weights session to improve the muscles of the upper body and to increase power through shots, whereas a marathon runner may use weights on the lower body to improve muscular endurance in the legs.

Safety

Weight training should follow many safety guidelines:

- The exercise should be completed correctly using the correct technique, e.g. the back should not be bent when picking weights up.
- If free weights are being used, a 'spotter' can be used to help in the initial lift, putting the weight down or to assist if the individual starts to struggle to lift the weight.

▲ A spotter assisting with safety.

- Children should not lift heavy weights as they can damage growing bones.
- A thorough warm up should be completed before lifting weights.
- A period of rest should follow every set (see overleaf for description of sets/reps).

> ✔ **Check your understanding**
>
> Can you remember what static stretching is and some advantages and disadvantages of using it?
>
> Answers are on page 177.

PRACTICE QUESTIONS

1. How are static stretches performed?   (2 marks)
2. How can the principle of specificity be applied when using static stretches?   (1 mark)

Answers are on page 180.

Calculating the correct intensity for weight training

As previously mentioned, weight training can be altered to suit the needs of an individual. In order to calculate the correct intensity, it is important that the person training knows what muscles they aim to train and how they wish to train them.

- One repetition (or rep) is completing one lift of the weight (up and down).
- One set is the completion of a number of reps.

In its simplest form, if an individual wishes to improve strength/power, they tend to lift heavy weights and complete few reps, but how do you calculate just how heavy the 'heavy' weights are?

One rep max

You may remember the one rep max test from earlier in the chapter. Calculating your one rep max is the first part of working out a suitable intensity of weight to lift. Once you know your one rep max you can adopt the following principles:

- **Strength/power training** involves lifting heavy weights with a low number of reps:
  - This involves lifting over 70 per cent of your one rep max with approximately three sets of 4–8 reps.
  - E.g. if a one rep max for bench press is 100 kg then the individual may well lift a 70 kg barbell, completing 3 sets of 6 reps (to improve strength).
- **Muscular endurance** involves lifting lighter weights with a high number of reps:
  - This involves lifting below 70 per cent of your one rep max with approximately three sets of 12–15 reps.
  - E.g. if a one rep max for bench press is 100 kg then the individual may well lift a 50 kg barbell, completing 3 sets of 15 repetitions.

N.B. Using your one rep max to help you calculate intensity also ensures that overload is occurring. Remember that the principles of training should always be applied so muscles being worked should be the ones usually used in the sport. Also, the choice of whether to calculate intensities for strength or muscular endurance will depend on the demand of the sport, e.g. marathon runners would tend to use muscular endurance whereas discus throwers would tend to need strength.

Advantages and disadvantages of weight training

Advantages of weight training:

- It can easily be adapted for different fitness aims, e.g. muscular strength or muscular endurance.
- It is relevant to all sports.
- It is relatively straightforward to carry out – you simply need something to lift.
- Strength gains can occur.

Rapid recall

Remember:
Strength: High weight/low rep
Muscular endurance: Low weight/ high rep

Activity

If you had a one rep max of 50 kg, how could you calculate intensity to improve muscular endurance?

Answer is on page 181.

Key terms

One repetition (or rep)
Completing one lift of a weight (up and down).

One set The completion of a number of reps.

Check your understanding

Calculate suitable sets and reps for strength and/or muscular endurance using one rep max.

Answers are on page 177.

Disadvantages of weight training:

- Heavy weights can increase blood pressure.
- Injury can occur if weights are too heavy or incorrect technique is used.
- Calculating one rep max requires high levels of motivation.

Safety principles when training

All training types must be completed with safety in mind. As a result, many factors must be considered to prevent injury. These are summarised below:

- The training type and the intensity used should match the training purpose, e.g. training for aerobic sports may well use continuous training at 60–80 per cent of maximal heart rate.
- A warm up and cool down should be completed prior to and after training.
- Over training should be avoided, e.g. appropriate weights should be lifted.
- Appropriate clothing and footwear should be worn which protect/support and allow movement.
- Taping/bracing should be used as necessary to protect and support areas of weakness.
- Hydration should be maintained with fluid intake.
- Stretches should not be overstretched or bounce.
- Technique used should be correct, e.g. lifting technique.
- Appropriate rest should be given in between sessions to allow for recovery.
- Spotters should be used when weight training if heavy weights are being attempted.

Specific training technique (high altitude training)

One specific training type used by elite athletes is that of high altitude training. High altitude training involves carrying out training at high altitude, i.e. high above sea level. Many athletes need to travel to different parts of the world in order to gain access to appropriate training areas at appropriate heights. High altitude training is a form of aerobic training, i.e. it trains the aerobic energy system and can improve a person's cardio-vascular endurance.

PRACTICE QUESTIONS

1. How is weight training intensity calculated to improve muscular endurance? (2 marks)
2. Using a sport of your choice, why might a performer use weight training to improve strength? (2 marks)

Answers are on page 180.

▲ Taping or bracing may be required when training.

Rapid recall

The word SAFER can be used to remember aspects of safety when training:
S – Stretches should be completed as part of a thorough warm up
A – Appropriate intensity should be used
F – Footwear and clothing should be appropriate to allow support/movement
ER – Exercise and rest – allow appropriate rest in between exercise sessions

Activity

In twos, without using your books, see how many training safety considerations you can remember.

How high altitude training is carried out:

- The individual trains at a high altitude – usually 2000 m or more above sea level.
- There is less oxygen in the air at high altitude. This makes training very difficult as the body finds it harder to carry oxygen to the working muscles.
- As a result, the body compensates by making more red blood cells to carry what oxygen there is in the air.

Therefore in simple terms:

As there is a very limited amount of oxygen in the air at altitude, training is very hard.

As a result, the human body makes more red blood cells to help carry the oxygen which is available.

Therefore, by the end of the training, the body has more red blood cells.

If the athlete then returns to sea level they will have:
More red blood cells
AND
The air will contain more oxygen at sea level

SO
They can carry vast amounts of oxygen, helping them to perform aerobic/endurance activities.

In summary, altitude training benefits:

- endurance athletes – e.g. marathon runners
- athletes that work aerobically – i.e. athletes that sustain exercise over a long period of time.

Altitude training has virtually no benefit for anaerobic athletes.

Study hint
Altitude does not however have any benefit for athletes who perform anaerobic exercise, e.g. sprinters, discus throwers.

▲ Altitude training increases red blood cell count.

High altitude training is a specific form of training and is complex in that many athletes need to travel to train in a foreign country. It has many limitations/negative effects:

- It can be very difficult to complete training. Some people find it too hard and actually train less than if they were at sea level.
- This means that fitness can actually be lost.
- Some athletes can suffer from altitude sickness – a feeling of nausea.
- The benefits are lost quite quickly – i.e. when returning to sea level, red blood cell count starts to decrease again.

The three training seasons

Although not all sports follow distinctive seasonal patterns, there are three 'traditional' parts to the training season which are still followed by many performers:

- pre-season (also known as preparation)
- competition season (also known as peak/playing season)
- post-season (also known as transition).

Each of the traditional training seasons have common aims and objectives:

- Pre-season/preparation – the aim is to improve general and aerobic fitness. This is often done via aerobic training, e.g. long runs. It is also an aim to improve specific fitness needs so that the performer is ready for competitive season, e.g. agility for tennis. A swimmer may well undertake long duration swims, before working on specific aspects of their technique. Similarly a cyclist may attempt to increase their general and aerobic fitness on a bike, whilst also working on specific skill aspects like climbing.
- Competition/peak/playing season – the aim is to maintain fitness levels. The performer should be at peak fitness and will aim to maintain this. They may well also work on specific skills used in their sport.
- Post-season/transition – the aim is to rest and recover from the season. Many performers also continue some light aerobic training so that fitness levels do not drop too far.

▲ Long, enduring runs may be included as part of pre-season training to improve aerobic fitness levels for activities that require running. The method of building up general aerobic fitness should be specific to the sport, e.g. cycling for a cyclist.

 Check your understanding

Describe positives and negatives of training at altitude.

Study hint

You may be required to explain the basics of altitude training – less oxygen at altitude, body compensates by making more red blood cells, etc. However, you do not need to know how to calculate intensities for training at altitude.

PRACTICE QUESTIONS

1. Would altitude training be used by a sprinter? Justify your answer. (2 marks)
2. What negative effects can altitude training have? (3 marks)

Answers are on page 180.

Study hint

It is a common mistake that students confuse the word 'seasons' with Spring, Summer, Autumn, Winter. Remember that seasons refer to pre-season, competition season and post-season.

Rapid recall

For the training seasons, remember PA CMA TRA
PA – **P**re-season, Build **a**erobic fitness
CMA – **C**ompetition, **M**aintain **A**erobic fitness
TRA – **T**ransition, **R**est, Small amounts of **a**erobic work

PRACTICE QUESTION

What is the main aim of the post-season/transition section of training? (1 mark)

Answer is on page 180.

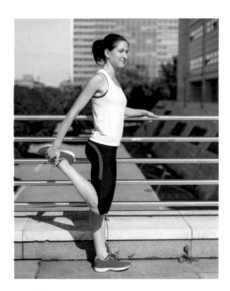

▲ Warming up.

Effective use of warm up and cool down

Warming up and cooling down are two very important aspects that a performer must consider to help prevent injury or ill effects of exercising.

Warming up

There are several parts that a good warm up should include in order to be fully effective:

- gradual pulse raising activity – e.g. fast walk/jog/light swim to increase the amount of oxygen to the working muscles
- stretching – of all relevant muscles
- skill-based practices/familiarisation activities, e.g. ball work in football
- mental preparation – starting to get focused, using techniques to control arousal, e.g. deep breathing.

By completing these parts of a warm up, the individual will benefit in the following ways:

- Body temperature will increase ready for exercise.
- Stretching will increase the range of movement possible.
- There will be a gradual (not over demanding) increase in effort towards 'competition pace', i.e. you gradually work up to the intensity required for the game/event.
- You will be focused and psychologically prepared.
- Movement skills that will be used have been practised before starting the game/match/event.
- There will be less chance of suffering injury.
- There will be an increase in the amount of oxygen being carried to the working muscles – helping with the production of energy.

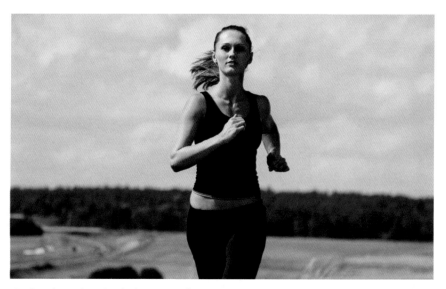

▲ A pulse raiser is vital as part of a warm up.

Cooling down

Performing a cool down is often overlooked and under-valued by sports performers. However, it holds a high level of importance and should not be ignored. An effective cool down should include:

- an activity to maintain an elevated breathing and heart rate, e.g. walk, jog
- a gradual reduction in intensity, e.g. jog to light jog to walk
- stretching of all main muscles used in the activity.

The benefits of cooling down can summarised as follows:

- It allows the body to start to recover after exercising.
- It helps with the removal of lactic acid, carbon dioxide and waste products.
- It can help to prevent the delayed onset of muscle soreness, sometimes referred to as DOMS.

▲ Cooling down should include some stretches.

> **Activity**
>
> In twos, design a suitable warm up and cool down for a sport of your choice.

PRACTICE QUESTIONS

1. What are the main components of a good warm up? (3 marks)
2. Identify two benefits of cooling down. (2 marks)

Answers are on page 180–181.

Rapid recall

The benefits of warming up can be remembered by using **TIMO**
T – Temperature increases
I – Injury chances reduce
M – Mental preparation
O – Oxygen to the working muscles (more)

Similarly, the benefits of cooling down can be remembered using **R COMS**
R – (Start to) recover gradually
C – Carbon dioxide removed
OMS – Onset of muscle soreness reduced

> ✔ **Check your understanding**
>
> Describe the parts of an effective warm up and cool down.

Study hint
Remember: It is important that a cool down should allow the body to gradually slow down. Intensity of exercise should be gradually reduced.

Summary

- There is some relationship between health and fitness but fitness does not guarantee being healthy (and vice versa)
- Performers in sporting activities need various components of fitness, but these vary in importance from sport to sport
- Fitness testing can: help you to develop a training programme, evaluate strengths and weaknesses, assist in the setting of goals and prevent tedium
- When carrying out fitness tests the correct procedures and safety considerations must be followed
- Quantitative data refers to quantities or numbers/facts
- Qualitative data refers to the quality of something. It is an opinion
- The principles of training should be applied when undertaking any training programme: specificity, progressive overload, reversibility, tedium
- The principles of overload should be applied when undertaking any training programme: frequency, intensity, time and type
- Suitable training types should be chosen to develop the desired components of fitness, relevant to the sport
- Warming up and cooling down should be part of any training session

Chapter 4 Sports psychology

Chapter objectives

- What is a skill and what is an ability?
- Classification of skills
- Definitions of types of goals
- The use and evaluation of setting performance and outcome goals in sporting examples
- The use of SMART targets to improve and/or optimise performance
- Basic information processing model
- Examples of and evaluation of the effectiveness of the use of types of guidance with reference to beginners and elite level performers
- Examples of and evaluation of the effectiveness of the use of types of feedback with reference to beginners and elite level performers
- Arousal and the inverted U theory
- How optimal arousal levels vary according to the skill being performed in a physical activity or sport
- How arousal can be controlled using stress management techniques before or during a sporting performance
- Understand the difference between direct and indirect aggression with application to specific sporting examples
- Understand the characteristics of introvert and extrovert personality types, including examples of sports which suit these particular personality types
- Intrinsic and extrinsic motivation as used in sporting examples

What is a skill and what is an ability?

As part of GCSE Physical Education, you need to understand the difference in meaning of the words **skill** and **ability**. Although these terms are sometimes used in the same way by sports commentators on television, they do in fact mean different things.

Skills are learned and, when mastered, are consistently done in a way that looks easy and uses the correct technique. Although skills can be mental (thinking skills) we tend to think of sporting skills as physical, for example passing a netball or shooting in basketball.

Abilities are inherited. They are known as 'traits' which remain fairly stable during your life. Balance, agility and co-ordination are examples of abilities you are born with. Abilities can help performers learn skills, for example greater inherited balance will help a gymnast learn the skills required on a balance beam.

Key terms

Skills A learned action/behaviour with the intention of bringing about predetermined results with maximum certainty and minimum outlay of time and energy.

Abilities Inherited from your parents, abilities are stable traits that determine an individual's potential to learn or acquire skills.

Rapid recall

The word ski**ll** has two 'L's. The word ability only has one. The one with the most **L**'s is the one that has to be **Learned**.

▲ A gymnast showing incredible balance (ability).

▲ A rugby player performing the skill of passing.

79

▲ The skill of free throw shooting in basketball. Skills are actions which must be learned.

Study hint
You should be able to choose and justify the appropriate classifications in relation to sporting examples.

✔ Check your understanding

What is a skill and what is an ability?

Answers are on page 182.

Classification of skills

You are not able to perform sporting skills immediately when you are born; they must be learned. In learning how to perform skills in sport (such as a pass or a dribble in hockey) performers tend to learn the basic skill first followed by more advanced versions.

For example, you may learn how to simply kick a ball first. Then you may learn how to strike a ball with some power using the laces, before learning how to bend a ball with the inside or outside of the foot.

Skill classification

To understand skilled actions in sport, it can help to classify skills into categories or groups. This is called skill classification and allows us to better understand basic, commonly performed skills. In doing so, skills can be positioned or placed onto continua (lines). These skill classification lines are called:

- The **basic** to **complex** continuum.
- The **open** to **closed** continuum.
- The **self-paced** to **externally-paced** continuum.
- The **gross** to **fine** continuum.

The basic to complex continuum

In deciding where a sporting skill falls on the basic to complex continuum certain factors must be considered:

- Who the skill is being taught to; for example, a beginner or a more experienced performer?
- How much decision making is involved – do you have to use high level thinking?
- Are the movements easy to carry out without much experience?

Basic ————————————————————————— Complex

BASIC SKILL	COMPLEX SKILL
Few decisions to be made.	Complex decision making.
Few decisions actually affect the success of the movement.	Lots of decisions to be made in order to be successful.
Tend to be taught as a beginner. Learned fairly quickly.	Tend to be taught after experiencing success in basic skills.
Walking is a basic skill.	Can take considerable time to master.
Jumping is a basic skill.	High jump is a complex skill requiring co-ordinated running in an accurate bend, followed by a correctly timed jump and effective body position to clear the bar.

▲ A forward roll is basic.

Activity

Looking at the pictures opposite with a partner, try to classify the skills forward roll and double somersault as either basic or complex skills. In doing so make sure you can explain your choice to each other.

Answers are on page 185.

The open to closed continuum

In deciding where a sporting skill falls on the open to closed continuum certain factors must be considered:

- What is going on in the environment when performing the skill?
- Is the environment stable – is it changing or not?
- Do other people affect how the skill might be done, for example opposition players?
- Do decisions need to be made as to how to do the skill because of things going on within the environment? For example, an opponent may try to tackle you in rugby so you change direction to avoid them.

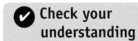

Open _____ Closed

OPEN SKILL	CLOSED SKILL
Unstable environment.	Stable environment.
The way you do the skill is affected by people around you.	The way you do the skill is not affected by people around you.
You may decide to do the skill differently to 'normal' because of the environment, for example what your opponents are doing,	You will not change how you do the skill. It is done the same way every time because there are no factors/people within the environment to affect how you do it.
The skill is often externally paced.	The skill is typically self-paced.
Examples:	Examples:
A football pass may be carried out in a certain way to avoid oncoming opponents, for example passed round them or chipped over them.	A somersault in gymnastics. You would try to replicate/repeat the skill in the same way as you do not need to change how you do it.
A rugby tackle may need to be performed in a certain way to catch and stop a moving opponent, for example if they get past you the tackle becomes a rear tackle rather than a front tackle.	A javelin throw is replicated each time. There is nothing to affect the direction of throw.
Both skills have been performed in a certain way because of opposition players. They may be performed differently next time.	The way you carry out these skills is not affected by factors or people around you (in the environment). You aim to carry these out the same way each time.

▲ A double somersault is more complex.

Key terms

Open skill A skill which is performed in a certain way to deal with a changing or unstable environment, e.g. to outwit an opponent.

Closed skill A skill which is not affected by the environment or performers within it. It tends to be done the same way each time.

> ✔ **Check your understanding**
>
> Can you remember how to determine if a skill is basic or complex?
>
> Answers are on page 182.

Study hint

The environment does NOT refer to the weather. It refers to the situation in which the skill is being performed, for example who is there, what they are doing etc.

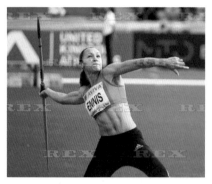

▲ Jessica Ennis-Hill throwing the javelin.

The photo shows Jessica Ennis-Hill performing a javelin throw. She aims to repeat the action of the throw each time. Nothing in the environment changes how it is done. She does not have to react to 'opponents' when throwing. It is repeatable and self-paced. It is therefore a closed skill.

PRACTICE QUESTIONS

1. What is the difference between a skill and an ability?   (1 mark)

2. Classify the following skills as either open or closed. In doing so make sure you can explain your choice.

- A shot in football during open play.
- A pass/setting in volleyball.
- A forward roll in gymnastics.
- A high jump.
- A goalkeeper trying to save a penalty flick in hockey.

(5 marks)

Answers are on page 183.

✓ Check your understanding

What makes a skill open or closed?

Answers are on page 182.

Study hint

If **you** (and nobody/nothing else) control when you start a movement and/or how fast the movement is, it is self-paced.

Key terms

Self-paced skill The skill is started when the performer decides to start it. The speed, rate or pace of the skill is controlled by the performer.

Externally-paced skill The skill is started because of an external factor. The speed, rate or pace of the skill is controlled by external factors, e.g. an opponent.

The self-paced to externally-paced continuum

In deciding where a sporting skill falls on the self-paced to externally-paced continuum certain factors must be considered:

- Who or what controls when the movement/skill should start?
- Who or what controls the speed, rate or pace at which the movement/skill is performed?

Self-paced Externally-paced

SELF-PACED SKILL	EXTERNALLY-PACED SKILL
The start of the movement is controlled by the performer.	The start of the movement is controlled by external factors.
For example, when performing a long jump, you choose when to start the run up.	For example, when receiving a badminton serve, you only start your returning shot after your opponent has performed their serve.
The speed, pace or rate of the movement is controlled by you.	The speed, pace or rate of the movement is controlled by external factors.
For example, when running a long distance race, you decide how fast to run.	For example, when marking an opponent in netball, your movement is affected by the movement of your opponent.

Match sprint velodrome cycling.

Pole vault.

✔ Check your understanding

What makes a skill self-paced or externally-paced?

Answers are on page 182.

In match sprint velodrome cycling, two cyclists cycle head to head over three laps of the track. They usually go slow for most of the race but have to respond if their opponent starts to sprint. Responding to your opponent's speed would make the skill externally-paced.

In pole vault you control how fast you run up. This is self-paced.

The gross to fine continuum

In deciding where a sporting skill falls on the gross to fine continuum certain factors must be considered:

- How much of the body is being used to perform the skill?
- Are large groups of muscles being used or small muscle groups?

Gross _____ Fine

GROSS SKILL	FINE SKILL
Involves big movements of the body.	Involves small, precise movements.
Involves the use of large muscle groups.	Involves the use of small muscle groups.
Movements tend not to rely on accuracy and precision, for example kicking a ball, running, throwing a javelin.	Movements tend to involve precision and accuracy, for example dart throw, archery, snooker, table tennis block shot.

A rugby tackle involves large muscle groups and is a gross skill.

A net shot in badminton requires precision and only a small movement of the wrist. It is a fine skill.

Activity

In pairs, try to classify the following skills as either self-paced or externally-paced skills. In doing so make sure you can explain your choice.

- A javelin throw.
- A sprint start.
- A conversion (kick) in rugby.

Answers are on page 185.

Study hint

Large movements of the body tend to be gross skills whereas small, precise movements tend to be fine skills.

✔ Check your understanding

What makes a skill gross or fine?

Answers are on page 182.

PRACTICE QUESTION

Javelin is an athletic event involving a run and throw. Classify a javelin throw as either gross or fine. Justify your answer. (2 marks)

Answer is on page 183.

▲ A sprinter may have a performance goal of getting a good start.

Key terms

Performance goals Personal standards to be achieved. The performer compares their performance against what they have already done or suggests what they are going to do. There is no comparison with other performers.

Outcome goals Focus on end result, for example winning.

Goal setting

In order to improve or to provide motivation, sports performers often set themselves goals or have goals set by their coaches. Goal setting gives performers a target to aspire to and helps to prepare performers both physically and mentally.

Although goals generally follow the principles of SMART goals (see below), for GCSE there are generally two types of goal which can be considered by performers/coaches:

- performance goals
- outcome goals.

Performance goals

A performance goal does not involve the performer comparing themselves to other performers. They simply compare themselves against what they have already done or suggest what they are going to do.

For example, a 100 m runner:

- may hope for a better start than the last race
- may aim to time their 'dip' well when crossing the line (better than last time).

Outcome goals

Outcome goals are simply used to judge the end result. They usually involve comparison with other competitors. The performance standards may not be that important. It is the outcome that matters.

For example, a football player:

- may wish to win the match
- may wish to score two goals to increase their team's goal difference.

The use of performance and outcome goals

Performers should really set themselves short term and long term goals. In doing so they have targets to achieve and can remain motivated to achieve their next goal.

However, it is important to realise that performance and outcome goals (used together) might not always be beneficial for all performers. Although they can be combined, it is generally accepted that beginners may be better avoiding outcome goals as they rely on factors that cannot be controlled, for example other performers.

Beginners (usually) prefer to avoid outcome goals as failure could demotivate them. It might be that winning may be an unrealistic goal for some performers. Beginners may be better concentrating on performance goals and trying to better themselves without worrying about the result compared to others.

On the other hand, elite athletes are sometimes driven by one thing and one thing only – winning! The use of performance goals can help to motivate them to work on individual aspects of performance, but the outcome goal of winning, or gaining a medal, may increase their desire to succeed even more. The best performers can persist, even when they fail, and become even more determined to succeed next time.

As Olympic champion, long jumper Greg Rutherford was under extreme pressure to perform well at the Glasgow 2014 Commonwealth Games. In terms of an outcome goal, it was simple for Greg – he wanted to win, stating 'That's what it's all about for me'. He achieved this outcome goal by winning a gold medal.

However, in the lead up to the event, Rutherford was also known to have set himself performance goals to drive hard in the sprint and stay tall at take-off.

PRACTICE QUESTION

Complete the table below. What performance and outcome goals could be set for the badminton beginner and elite javelin thrower?

(4 marks)

A complete beginner playing badminton against a more experienced player	Performance goal:	Outcome goal:
An elite level javelin thrower performing at the Olympic Games	Performance goal:	Outcome goal:

Answers on page 183.

Study hint
Performance goals are more appropriate than outcome goals for beginners.

SMART target setting

It is generally accepted that whatever goals are set, they should follow the SMART principles. The goal should be:

S – Specific (specific to the demands of the sport/muscles used/ movements involved).

M – Measureable (it must be possible to measure whether it has been achieved).

A – Accepted (it must be accepted/agreed by the performer and the performer's coach, if they have one).

R – Realistic (it must actually be possible to complete the goal, that the person is physically capable).

T - Time-bound (it must be set over a fixed period of time).

> **Activity**
>
> With a partner or in small groups, try to explain what each part of SMART stands for. You could take a letter each to start with and do this as a 'Mexican wave' around the table.
>
> Answers are on page 185.

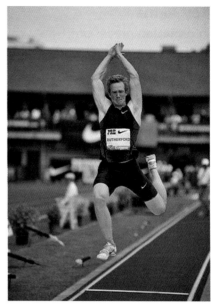

▲ Greg Rutherford, Olympic long jump champion in 2012.

 Check your understanding

What is the difference between a performance and an outcome goal?

Answers are on page 182.

▲ Performers who have a SMART goal to achieve tend to be motivated to achieve it and persist in their attempts to accomplish it.

Key terms

Information processing This is making decisions. It involves gathering data from the display (senses) and prioritising the most important stimuli to make a suitable decision, for example choosing a suitable skill.

A basic model of information This shows the simple processes that a performer carries out in order to decide what skill to use.

Basic model of information processing

Having looked at what a skill is earlier in this chapter, it is now important to understand how skills are chosen and how decisions are made.

Information processing is using available information in order to make a decision; this is choosing a suitable skill or movement.

In choosing an appropriate skill to use in sport, you also have to decide how to use it.

Beginners tend to attempt to perform a skill the same way every time whereas elite sportspeople are able to vary how they use skills.

For example, a beginner serving a tennis ball may simply try to serve it. They have one serve that they can use, so attempt it and hope that it goes in. Elite players can serve a tennis ball in many ways. They can serve with speed, with spin, etc.

▲ In a penalty kick the performer will choose *how* to kick the ball, for example with power, with placement etc.

▲ Elite players have a vast array of serves that they use when performing.

Study hint

You need to be able to draw the information processing model (right). You may also have to say what happens at each stage of the model.

As you can see from the model there are four parts to the diagram – input, decision making, output and feedback.

Activity

Try to draw the various stages of an information processing model and fill in the names of each stage.

Answers are on page 185.

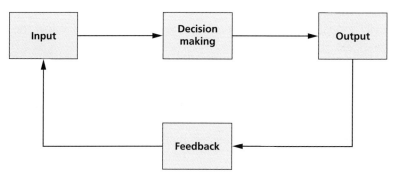

▲ Basic model of information processing.

Input:

- Performer takes in information from the environment/display (for example, what they can see, what they can hear, what they can feel).
- They choose what is the most relevant signal/cue/stimulus/piece of information to them at that time.
- For example, sight when watching a cricket ball flying through the air. This is called selective attention. It is a fitering process whereby they pick out the most important parts of the display that are relevant and discard those that are not.

Decision making:

- This is where the performer selects an appropriate response (movement/skill) from memory; perhaps one they have used in this situation before.
- The short-term memory (STM) is the 'working memory'. Information from the display that has been attended to is held in the short-term memory for a short time (approx. 30 seconds). If your attention is directed to something else, the information is lost.
- The long-term memory (LTM) holds information that has been rehearsed and stored. Thus if a memory or past experience is relevant to what is required at that time, it is compared to information in the short-term memory so that a suitable decision can be made.
- The cricketer may have attended to the sight of a ball in the air. He/she recalls the memory of a previous catch (from LTM) and compares it to what he/she is currently seeing (STM) so that the decision to catch can take place.

Output:

- The decision chosen is sent to the appropriate muscles to carry out the response.
- For example, impulses sent to arms and hands to start the appropriate muscular movements for the catch to take place.

Feedback:

- Information is received via themselves (intrinsic) and/or from others (extrinsic) regarding the success (or not) of the action.
- Note, the feedback received may affect how you complete this skill in the future.
- For example, you can feel the ball in the hands (intrinsic) and your team mates cheer when you catch it (extrinsic).

Activity

Try to suggest the stages of a basic information processing model for a sporting skill of your choice. We have completed one for you below.

✓ Check your understanding

What are the four stages of information processing?

Answers are on page 182.

PRACTICE QUESTIONS

1. What do you understand by the term 'selective attention'? (1 mark)
2. Explain the 'input' stage of information processing. (2 marks)

Answers are on page 184.

Guidance

Having already performed or whilst learning how to perform a skill, performers need help from their coach or teacher in order to improve. Such help may come in the form of **guidance**.

There are four types of guidance:

- Visual (being shown something)
- Verbal (hearing something/instructions)
- Manual (assistance with the movement – physical)
- Mechanical (use of objects/aids).

In order to choose what type of guidance to use, the biggest factor to consider is the experience level of the performer. A beginner is obviously in need of guidance to allow them to learn and progress. However, an elite, experienced performer may also require guidance to fine tune performance or stop minor errors.

Study hint

Make sure you are able to identify appropriate examples of guidance for beginners and elite level performers.

Key term

Visual guidance Guidance that you can see, for example a demonstration.

Visual guidance

Visual guidance is simply when the performer can see something. For example, a coach, teacher or fellow performer may well show them something.

Visual guidance includes:

- demonstration of technique or skill by another person, for example the coach
- footage of performance via DVD, analysis software, slow motion, different angles
- still images, for example posters or photographs.

For a beginner, visual guidance is very important so that they can see and start to understand what they are expected to do. If a coach explains a new skill to a performer for the first time, they will benefit from seeing it first. Verbal guidance may not be enough for a beginner without also getting to see the skill.

Demonstrations for beginners will only work if they are:

- clear
- relatively concise
- quick
- easy to understand
- of a realistic standard for the beginner to copy or aim towards
- backed up with simplistic verbal guidance (allowing the performer to concentrate on the main points).

▲ A coach uses visual guidance to show performers how the skill should be done.

▲ The golf coach manually guides the young golfer to help her use the correct technique.

For elite performers, visual guidance is not used as much. However it can be used to highlight minor errors in technique via analysis software or slow motion. It is combined with verbal guidance as the performer is able to understand complex terminology.

Verbal guidance

Verbal guidance is commonly used with visual guidance. It involves another person (usually a coach or teacher) telling the learner what they are doing right or wrong. It can also be used as a key word trigger, for example 'point your toes'.

Verbal guidance may involve:

- a coach/teacher talking to a performer, highlighting technique
- a coach/teacher highlighting a key 'trigger point', for example 'and push' when a performer hits the trampoline.

Verbal guidance will only work for beginners if:

- it actually relates to the visual guidance being given
- it is not too long or complex, that is they can understand it.

Verbal guidance can work with elite performers. It might:

- be longer and more complex than for beginners
- not need to be supplemented with visual guidance as elite performers are likely to know what the skill should look like.

Manual/mechanical guidance

Manual and mechanical guidance are very similar and can be grouped together. They involve either physically moving the performer, for example the coach supporting the movement through physical touch, or using mechanical aids, for example arm bands. The physical support or use of mechanical aids allows the performer to produce the required movement when they may not have been able to do it by themselves.

Manual/mechanical guidance may involve:

- physically guiding the performer, for example the coach moving the learner's arm through the correct motion of a forehand drive
- supporting the performer for safety, so that the required movement takes place, e.g. supporting a gymnast whilst trying to do a vault.

Key term

Verbal guidance Guidance that is provided by another person speaking to you.

Key terms

Manual guidance Physically moving the performer, for example the coach supporting the movement through physical touch.

Mechanical guidance Using mechanical aids to assist a performer, for example using a float in swimming or a harness in trampolining.

⏶ Beginners are likely to need visual guidance first with simple verbal instructions. They may also need manual/mechanical guidance.

Sporting examples include:

- the use of arm bands (mechanical)
- the use of a trampoline harness (mechanical)
- holding a perfomer's wrist in tennis to guide them through the movement of a forehand shot (manual)
- standing behind a golfer at the driving range and holding their hands through a golf swing (manual).

Manual/mechanical guidance can be useful for beginners because:

- it can help the beginner feel safe/supported
- it can help the beginner complete the required movement for a skill
- it can help the performer to start to understand how a movement should feel (intrinsic feedback).

However, manual/mechanical guidance must be used to develop the correct movement as mistakes in technique (as a result of using manual/mechanical guidance) might start to become the normal learned response. Manual/mechanical guidance should not be used for too long as performers can become reliant upon them. Elite performers do not usually require manual or mechanical guidance unless unexpected flaws in technique start to occur.

Differences between beginners and elite performers:

BEGINNERS	ELITE PERFORMERS
Definitely need visual guidance to understand what a skill looks like.	Are unlikely to need visual guidance other than to highlight minor faults, for example use of slow motion.
Also need verbal guidance but it should not be too long or complex.	Will need verbal guidance. It is likely to be longer and more complex than that given to a beginner. It allows 'fine-tuning' of technique.
Are also likely to need manual/mechanical guidance to support or guide through the correct technique.	Elite performers are unlikely to need manual/mechanical guidance unless there is an unexpected flaw in technique.

- Visual guidance is used more for beginners.
- Verbal guidance is used more for elite performers.
- Mechanical guidance is used more for beginners.

Beginners are likely to need visual guidance first with simple verbal instructions. They may also need manual/mechanical guidance.

Feedback

Feedback is simply information that a performer receives. It can be received before, during or after performance and can come from a variety of sources:

- from within (intrinsic)
- from others (extrinsic)
- from results/scores (extrinsic).

The varying types of feedback are:

- positive/negative
- knowledge of results/knowledge of performance
- extrinsic/intrinsic.

In choosing the correct type of feedback to use it is important that the experience of the performer is taken into account. Unlike experienced performers beginners are unable to make use of the feedback received.

Positive and negative feedback

Positive and negative feedback are of course opposites. Both are given by other people (extrinsically), for example coach, teacher, fellow performer.

Positive feedback is used to inform the athlete what was correct about the movement. Performers need to know if a movement is correct as this provides the reference point for future attempts at the movement. Positive feedback is essential in motivating athletes.

Negative feedback is used to inform the athlete what was incorrect about the movement. Negative feedback must include information on the action(s) required by the performer to achieve the correct movement.

Knowledge of results/knowledge of performance

Knowledge of results is sometimes known as 'KR'. It focuses on how successful you have been in achieving what you set out to do (the outcome). It is generally factual and given to you by a coach or teacher, although you may be able to see it yourself, for example the distance you jumped in long jump.

Examples include:

- whether you scored or not with a free throw in basketball
- what score you recorded in golf
- whether your shot in football went in the goal or not
- how quickly you ran the 100 metres.

Knowledge of results may be obvious to an elite athlete, but a beginner may need this type of feedback to understand whether what they did was a success or not.

Knowledge of performance, on the other hand, provides more detail about how well you did irrespective of the result. It may relate to technique used, or specific aspects of the movement you produced. It deals with the quality of the performance, not the result.

▲ Positive feedback is important for beginners to keep them motivated.

Study hint

Positive feedback is more important for beginners. Negative feedback tends to be used more with elite performers.

Key term

Knowledge of results (KR)
Feedback about the outcome.

Key term

Knowledge of performance
Feedback about the quality of performance, for example technique.

Examples include:

- The technique used when performing a free throw – 'excellent elbow extension'.
- 'Your swing was excellent in that golf shot' – 'great balance'.
- 'Excellent power through the laces' when shooting at goal in football.
- Quick out of the blocks in 100 metres with high knee lift.

Extrinsic/intrinsic feedback

Extrinsic feedback is information received about performance which comes from outside of the performer, for example from a coach or teacher. Extrinsic feedback may also come from fellow performers or the spectators and is generally given verbally, or it could be given on a score card, for example a score out of 10 in ice skating. As beginners often struggle to understand or interpret the success of their movement, they rely heavily on feedback from others.

▲ An elite performer like Rory McIlroy is able to give himself feedback. He will know from intrinsic 'feel' if his golf shot has been struck well or not.

Key terms

Intrinsic feedback Feedback from within, for example kinaesthetic feel.

Extrinsic feedback Feedback from an external source.

Intrinsic feedback is information which is received from within the performer, for example how something feels, information from the senses or muscles. As performers progress and become elite, they develop the ability to interpret such sensory information. In effect, they can 'feel' if a skill has been performed well. This 'feeling' or sense that the movement of the muscles and joints has gone well (or not) is often called kinaesthesis.

For example:

- An elite golfer will know from the 'feel' of their swing if it was a good shot.
- An elite hockey player will know from the 'feel' of their shot at goal if they have struck it well or not.
- An elite tennis player will know from the 'feel' of their serve as to whether they have generated enough spin on the ball.

BEGINNER	ELITE PERFORMER
May be demotivated by negative feedback.	More accepting of negative feedback.
Cannot interpret complex feedback on performance.	Can interpret complex feedback on performance.
Cannot provide themselves with feedback.	Can provide themselves with feedback.

PRACTICE QUESTIONS

1. What type of guidance is most important for beginners? (1 mark)
2. Why should negative feedback not be used excessively with beginners? (1 mark)
3. A beginner new to the sport requires feedback on their first attempt at hitting a hockey ball. Should Knowledge of Results or Knowledge of Performance be given? Justify your answer. (2 marks)

Answers are on page 184.

Answers are on page 184.

Rapid recall

Beginner REP, Elite PIN:

Beginner **REP** – Beginners are more suited to **R**esults (knowledge of), **E**xtrinsic and **P**ositive feedback.

Elite **PIN** – Elite performers are more suited to **P**erformance (knowledge of), **I**ntrinsic and **N**egative feedback.

The types of feedback can be remembered with '**REPPIN**':
R– Results (knowledge of)
E– Extrinsic
P– Positive
P– Performance (Knowledge of)
I – Intrinsic
N – Negative

Activity

You should be able to link the types of guidance and feedback to beginners and/or elite performers.

Try to complete the following table on your own or in a small group:

Beginner	Who requires the following and why?	Elite performer
	Visual guidance?	
	Verbal guidance?	
	Manual/mechanical guidance?	
	Positive or negative feedback?	
	Knowledge of results/performance?	
	Extrinsic or intrinsic feedback?	

Answers are on page 185.

Answers are on page 185.

Study hint
Beginners tend to need positive feedback, knowledge of results and extrinsic feedback.
Elite performers tend to accept negative feedback, knowledge of performance and can provide themselves with informed, intrinsic feedback.

Arousal

Arousal is a physical and mental (physiological and psychological) state of alertness/excitement varying from deep sleep to intense excitement.

Deep sleep ———————————————————— Intense excitement

Low level of arousal ———————————— High level of arousal

Arousal affects both the physical and mental state of a performer. Physically, increases in arousal may cause a rise in heart rate or cause a performer to sweat more. As arousal increases, performers must use specific strategies to control the level of arousal as if arousal is not at the correct level, performance may suffer.

The Inverted U theory of arousal

Yerkes and Dobson (1908) developed a theory called the Inverted U theory which visually shows how a performer can be under or over aroused, or at the correct (optimal) level.

Check your understanding

What do you understand by the term 'arousal'?

Answers are on page 182.

Study hint

It is not a sporting example, but threading a needle requires a low optimal level of arousal as it is a precise movement which uses small muscle groups and requires accuracy. These are the main criteria for requiring a low level of arousal.

PRACTICE QUESTION

Explain how arousal affects performance according to the Inverted U theory. (3 marks)

Answers are on page 184.

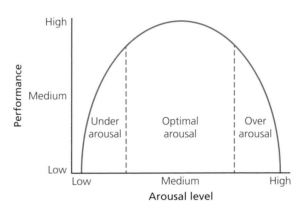

▲ The Inverted U theory.

The Inverted U theory can be explained in the following way:

- As arousal increases so does performance.
- Up to the optimal/perfect level.
- If arousal increases further, performance will decrease.

In order to understand this theory, you must understand that the optimal/perfect level of arousal varies for different sporting skills. For example:

- Fine/precise movements involving accuracy require a low optimal level of arousal.
- Gross/skills requiring power, strength and/or large muscle movements require a high level of arousal.

Low optimal level of arousal ——————— High optimal level of arousal

Fine/precise ———————————— Gross/large muscle movements

Archery ——————————————————— Rugby tackle

Snooker ——————————————————— Sprinting

Darts ——————————————————— Weightlifting

As different skills require different optimal levels of arousal, the Inverted U graph can be placed on different points of the graph according to the skill being performed. This is shown below:

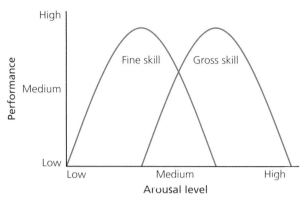

▲ Differing optimal levels of arousal for different skills.

Controlling arousal levels

Performers like Tom Daley need to control their arousal on a diving platform in order to ensure their performance is the best it can be. An incorrect level of arousal may result in mistakes being made as a result of under or over arousal.

▲ An archer who requires a low level of arousal could easily suffer from over arousal due to nerves or anxiety (worry).

▲ A weightlifter who does not get aroused enough may suffer from under arousal and be unable to lift the weight.

Methods to control arousal can be in the mind (mental/cognitive) or through use of the body (physical/somatic). The main methods that sports performers use are:

- **deep breathing** (physical/somatic)
- mental rehearsal/visualisation/imagery (mental/cognitive)
- positive self-talk (mental/cognitive).

Deep breathing

Deep breathing is a physical/somatic technique which involves the performer exaggerating their breaths in and out. The top half of the body should be relaxed and slow, deep breaths should be used to allow the performer to control arousal and focus their thoughts on the task in hand. This can be used before performance to calm nerves and control arousal. It can also be used during performance to focus the mind on the task in hand.

▲ Cristiano Ronaldo is known to deep breathe in preparation for his free kicks. His pose and stance are repeated before each free kick, and deep, exaggerated breaths help him focus on the skill he is about to execute.

Key term

Deep breathing A physical/somatic technique which involves the performer exaggerating their breaths in and out.

▲ Jonny Wilkinson in his famous 'pose'.

Study hint

Remember that players can be under aroused or over aroused. If under aroused, performers may need some form of motivation to increase their arousal level.

✔ **Check your understanding**

What do you understand by the terms 'somatic technique' and 'mental technique'?

Answers are on page 182.

Key terms

Mental rehearsal A mental technique involving the performer picturing themselves performing the skill perfectly before attempting it. This mental/cognitive relaxation technique involves control of mental thoughts and imagining positive outcomes.

Self-talk A mental/cognitive technique whereby the performer talks to him/herself in their head to reassure themselves.

Mental rehearsal/visualisation/imagery

Mental rehearsal, visualisation and imagery are very similar techniques used by performers to control their arousal levels. These techniques are done in the performer's mind (mental/cognitive). Mental rehearsal involves the performer picturing themselves performing the skill perfectly before attempting it. This can also be classed as imagery, although imagery can also involve the performer imagining themselves in a calm, relaxing place. Both methods relax and focus the mind on the task in hand and can be used before and during performance to control arousal levels. Visualisation involves you imagining a relaxing scene or place.

Examples of when mental rehearsal could be used during performance include:

- control arousal prior to kicking a rugby conversion
- control arousal before playing a cricket shot
- control arousal prior to throwing a javelin.

Jonny Wilkinson famously adopted a 'pose' before converting a rugby ball. This pose has been copied by many other rugby players. However, the background to Jonny's pose is that he was deep breathing and mentally rehearsing his kick. He visualised the ball going between the posts. Jonny subsequently controlled his arousal levels and focused his mind on the task in hand.

Positive self-talk

Self-talk is a mental/cognitive technique whereby the performer talks to themselves in their head. This technique is usually positive and can reassure performers that they are doing well or are well prepared and can relax their body and mind, controlling their arousal level.

Examples of sports performers using positive self-talk could include:

- a golfer reassuring him/herself that he/she can hole a putt
- an athlete in the blocks confirming to themselves that they are good enough to win
- a netballer quietly encouraging herself to score, for example 'Come on, you can do this'.

Activity

Performers may use a mixture of techniques at different times but the key is to realise that the arousal level must be correct for the skill being done.

Analyse the information below and try to fill in the table:

Sporting situation	Arousal level	Do they need to control/adjust their arousal level?	If yes, suggest an appropriate technique
Archery	Medium		
Weightlifter	High		
Snooker player	High		

Answers are on page 186.

PRACTICE QUESTIONS

1. Name a mental/cognitive technique that could be used to control arousal. (1 mark)
2. If a sports performer was suffering from over arousal, name and explain a somatic technique that could be used to control their level of arousal. (2 marks)

Answers are on page 184.

Aggression

For the vast majority of sports, an element of aggression may be required in order to succeed or win.

It is first important to understand what aggression is. Acts of aggression can be classified as direct aggression or indirect aggression.

Direct aggression

Direct aggression is when there is actual physical contact between performers. The 'aggressor' uses physical contact to directly and deliberately inflict harm upon their opponent. Examples of direct aggression include:

- a high rugby tackle with force
- a judo performer throwing their opponent illegally and with excessive force
- a boxer punching their opponent below the belt.

Indirect aggression

Indirect aggression does not involve physical contact. The aggressive act is taken out on an object to gain an advantage over an opponent. They do not physically harm or injure and the act may be within the rules of the sport. The 'harm' as such is usually mental harm, that is it makes the opponent(s) feel less confident or worried. Examples include:

- smashing a badminton shuttle very hard to win a point but also harming the confidence of the opponent
- in tennis, hitting a volley with power to win the point (but also to lower the opponent's confidence).

> ✔ **Check your understanding**
>
> What is the difference between direct and indirect aggression?
>
> Answers are on page 182.

Study hint
Remember that acts of aggression can be classified as direct aggression or indirect aggression. It is important that you understand the difference between the two.

Study hint
Direct aggression involves physical contact. Indirect aggression does not.

PRACTICE QUESTION

A netball player catches a ball with their elbows pointing outwards, deliberately hitting their opponent's face. Is this act of aggression direct or indirect? Explain your answer. (2 marks)

Answers are on page 184.

Key terms

Extrovert Personality type characterised by being sociable, active, talkative and out-going – usually associated with team sports players.

Introvert Personality type characterised by being quiet, passive, reserved and shy – usually associated with individual sports performance.

▲ Archery is a sport often performed by introverts.

Introvert and extrovert personality types

Sports psychologists try to understand the personality of performers. The unique 'parts' of a person's personality distinguish them from other people. Everyone is different, but certain types of personality can be grouped into categories. Two commonly used personality 'types' are **introvert** and **extrovert**. The main things that classifies a person as introvert or extrovert are:

- how much arousal they need for optimal performance
- whether they need others around them to stimulate them.

Introvert

A person with an introvert personality does not need a high level of arousal. They can become over aroused when over stimulated. They tend to be shy, quiet, thoughtful and solitary.

Note: introverts tend to play individual sports as they are self-motivated and don't need others to motivate them.

Introverts tend to play individual sports when:

- concentration/precision (fine skill) is required
- low arousal is required.

Extrovert

A person with an extrovert personality needs a high level of arousal. They can lack concentration and often seek exciting situations. They tend to enjoy interaction with others, are sociable, are aroused by others, are often enthusiastic, talkative and prone to boredom when isolated.

Extroverts tend to play team sports when there is a fast pace, concentration may need to be low and gross skills are used.

Note: extroverts are often leaders within a team.

▲ Team sports performers tend to be extroverted. They seek out excitement with others and often make good leaders.

> ### Activity
>
> Look at the list of the following activities and descriptive words. Group them into the categories of stereotypical introvert or extrovert personality types.
>
> | Introvert | | Extrovert |
> | --- | --- | --- |
> | | Pistol shooting | |
> | | Shy | |
> | | Seek excitement | |
> | | Rugby player | |
> | | Snooker player | |
> | | Calm | |
> | | Sociable | |
>
> Answers are on page 186.

✔ Check your understanding

What is the difference between an introvert and an extrovert?

Answers are on page 183.

PRACTICE QUESTION

Multiple choice (choose one).

Which one of the following tends to describe an introvert personality?

- easily excited
- enjoys sociable occasions
- usually shy
- very talkative. (1 mark)

Answer is on page 184.

Motivation

Motivation is simply defined as the drive to succeed or the desire (want) to achieve something. What actually motivates you can be divided into two main categories:

Intrinsic motivation and **extrinsic motivation**.

Intrinsic motivation

Intrinsic motivation is the drive that comes from within the performer. The need to achieve something may well have the reward of a feeling of pride, self-satisfaction or general achievement. The performer is driven to achieve something for the feeling it brings them.

Key terms

Motivation The drive to succeed or the desire (want) to achieve something.

Intrinsic motivation The drive that comes from within the performer.

Extrinsic motivation The drive experienced by a performer when striving to achieve a reward (tangible or intangible).

Study hint

You may need to explain appropriate examples of intrinsic and extrinsic motivation linked to sporting examples.

✓ Check your understanding

What is motivation?

Answers are on page 183.

Rapid recall

The value of intrinsic motivation can be remembered with the acronym SUPER:

Stronger – Intrinsic generally believed to be stronger/better

Undermine – Overuse of extrinsic can undermine intrinsic value

Persist – More likely to persist if motivated intrinsically

Effort – Is more likely to be sustained if intrinsically motivated

Reliance – Performers can become too reliant on extrinsic motivation.

▲ The potential to win a trophy can provide extrinsic motivation. Winning it may provide intrinsic motivation, for example feelings of pride, self-satisfaction.

Extrinsic motivation

Extrinsic motivation is the drive experienced by a performer when striving to achieve a reward. The external reward is provided by an outside source or person. Such reward can be divided into:

- tangible rewards – such as certificates, trophies, medals, etc.
- intangible rewards – such as praise or feedback from others, applause from the crowd.

Evaluation of the merits of intrinsic and extrinsic motivation in sport

It would be wrong to think that intrinsic and extrinsic motivation are used in isolation to each other. They are usually used together, and although a trophy may act as an extrinsic motivator, the pride or satisfaction from winning may also be a major intrinsic motivator.

The majority of educational and sporting research has concluded that intrinsic motivation is more powerful than extrinsic motivation. Intrinsic motivation is generally deemed more effective for a variety of reasons:

- Performers can become too reliant on extrinsic motivation. They only play for the reward/prize/money.
- Intrinsic motivation is more likely to lead to continued effort and participation, that is a performer who is playing for pride is more likely to keep persisting and continue participating over a period of time.
- The overuse of extrinsic can undermine the strength of intrinsic. In other words, if too many rewards are on offer, it may cause performers to forget why they were playing in the first place, that is for the love of the game.

However, the value of extrinsic rewards should not be underestimated. Winning a prize, trophy or certificate may well spur a performer on and actually cause feelings of pride/self-satisfaction.

PRACTICE QUESTIONS

1. What do you understand by the term motivation? (1 mark)
2. What is the difference between intrinsic and extrinsic motivation? (2 marks)
3. Is intrinsic or extrinsic motivation generally regarded as the most beneficial? Explain your answer. (2 marks)

Answers are on page 184.

Summary

- Skills are learned and abilities are inherited
- Skills can be classified on continua depending on their characteristics
- Outcome goals involve the outcome whereas performance goals involve technique or mastery
- Outcome goals tend to be more effective with elite performers than beginners
- SMART targets are specific, measureable, agreed, realistic and time-bound
- Information processing is using information to make decisions. It involves input, decision making, output and feedback
- Decisions can come from the short-term memory or the long-term memory
- Feedback can be given in a variety of ways
- Guidance involves visual, verbal, manual/mechanical
- Some guidance types are better suited to beginners, e.g. visual, manual/mechanical
- Some guidance types are better suited to experts, e.g. verbal
- Arousal is an excitement level. The correct level of arousal varies from skill to skill
- Arousal can be controlled using stress management techniques
- Direct aggression involves physical contact with the intent to harm
- Introverts are shy, can arouse themselves and prefer individual sports. Extroverts need others to arouse them and prefer team sports

Chapter objectives

- Understand the engagement patterns of different social groups
- Understand the factors affecting participation

Participation

It has been government policy for the last 50 years to try to make sure that every individual in the country has the opportunity to participate in sport and other forms of physical activity.

▲ There are many forms of physical activity.

We have seen the building of sports halls, the provision of outdoor recreation and sports facilities, the opening up of the countryside, an ongoing information campaign and a focus within school physical education programmes on increasing participation. All of these efforts have been part of an attempt to get more people involved in physical activity and sport. Has it worked?

The most recent research (2013) suggests that:

- only 36 per cent of people participate in physically active sport.

The research also showed some differences in levels of participation between **social groups**:

- Only 17 per cent of people with a disability participate regularly in physical activity and sport
- Only 38 per cent of adults from black and other ethnic minority groups participate regularly in physical activity and sport
- Only 26 per cent from the lowest socio-economic groups participate regularly in physical activity and sport
- Male participation is 41 per cent; and female participation is 31 per cent.

The term used to describe how levels of participation vary across different social groups is called **engagement patterns**.

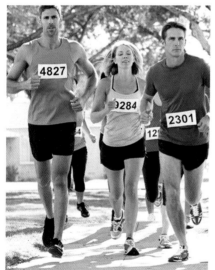

▲ There are many forms of physical activity.

Key terms

Social groups People who interact with one another, share similar characteristics, and have a sense of unity/togetherness.

Engagement patterns Trends/tendencies in involvement.

Social groups have a huge influence on people and will affect whether or not people become involved in sport and physical activity and which activities they become involved in.

One of the biggest factors that determines a person's engagement in physical activity is a person's gender.

▲ There are many forms of physical activity.

Participation by women

During the growth in sport and physical activity over the last 100 years, women's participation has been affected by a range of **stereotypical** views. For example:

- Women lack the strength or endurance to do the same range of sports or physical activities as men.
- Women who are competitive are not being feminine.
- Too much physical activity limits a women's ability to give birth.
- Women who train hard and develop muscles become more 'male-like' and have their sexual orientation questioned.
- A woman's role is to be the carer, mother and manager of the home and this prevents involvement in sport.

The majority of these **stereotypes** tend to be held by men about women, and although society is becoming more accepting of the idea of female sporting participation, there are many who still think along these lines.

Because of these stereotypical views, other **barriers to participation** have been put in place which put off women from participating in as wide a range of sports as men. For example:

- Sport is a male-dominated activity.
- Elite female sport performers receive less media coverage than men.
- Women receive less support from their peers and family.
- Facilities for women have developed more slowly than those for male performers.
- Media coverage of elite women performers is likely to include details that are not relevant to their performance – looks, attractiveness, whether they are married or have children, etc.

PRACTICE QUESTION

Discuss whether the opportunities for women to take part in sport and physical activity are the same as for men.   (4 marks)

Answer are on pages 187–188.

Key terms

Stereotype Widely held but fixed and oversimplified idea of a particular type of person.

Barrier to participation An obstacle that prevents a group within society from participating in sport or physical activity and therefore reduces overall levels of participation.

Participation by ethnicity

Ethnic group A community made up of people who share a common cultural background.

Another barrier to participation in physical activity is a person's race, religion or culture. An **ethnic group** is defined as a group of people who share common origins – be they racial, religious or cultural.

✔ Check your understanding

1 What are engagement patterns?
2 What do you understand by the term stereotypes?
3 Identify five ethnic groupings.
4 List four barriers to women's participation.

Answers are on page 187.

In the UK there is a wide variety of different ethnic minority groups. These groups have different levels of participation in sport and physical activity.

ETHNIC GROUP	AVERAGE LEVEL	BLACK CARIBBEAN	INDIAN	PAKISTANI	BANGLADESHI	BLACK AFRICAN	'BLACK OTHER'
Participation level % (men)	54	39	47	42	46	60	80
Participation level % (women)	39	34	31	24	19	34	45

The reasons for these differing levels of participation are linked to the different priorities and expectations of the groups.

There is also an unevenness of representation of different ethnic groups at elite levels of sport. For example, in the England football and the UK athletics squads, about 30 per cent of players are from ethnic minority communities. This compares to the general population in which about 13 per cent are from ethnic minorities.

The stereotypical response to these numbers is that people from Black Caribbean and African groups have better physiological or anatomical attributes due to their genetic make-up. They have an innate advantage.

Athletics and football often require speed, power and strength and it is suggested that these ethnic groups have a higher proportion of fast-twitch muscle fibres, or have a longer Achilles tendon allowing for greater power transfer or have a higher ratio of muscle to fat. The idea of a lower proportion of fat is also used to explain why there is a low representation of black people in competitive swimming.

There are many other sports that require similar physiological characteristics to athletics and football – for example, tennis, sprint cycling and rugby union – yet we do not see the same high representation there.

▲ Ethnic grouping is not a barrier to sports participation.

The imbalances that ethnic minorities have, both in levels of participation in sport and at an elite level, are due to a range of factors and are caused by several influences; there is no one single reason.

Other factors affecting participation

Surveys have shown that individuals from lower **socio-economic groups** are less likely to participate in physical activity. Many people from ethnic minority groups are also in lower socio-economic groups and therefore have less disposable income.

This may explain the high proportion of elite footballers and athletes from certain ethnic minority groups. These activities are relatively inexpensive to participate in, especially when compared to activities such as tennis or golf.

Socio-economics has an effect on participation in that participation invariably involves a cost to the participant. In the UK you 'pay to play', and some physical activities may cost a lot of money to play.

Another factor affecting participation in sport and physical activity is age. All school children participate in physical activity, because PE is a compulsory subject in schools. It is after children leave school that participation levels drop. There is a '**post-school drop-out**' in sport, especially among girls.

Not surprisingly, sports participation tends to be lower in older people than younger people, because many activities are restricted by physical fitness and as this declines with age, so participation levels drop. The type of activity undertaken also varies by age, with younger people more involved with team sports and older people more likely to be involved in individual activities.

PRACTICE QUESTION

Give **three** reasons for the lower participation rates among some ethnic minority groups.　　　(3 marks)

Answer is on page 188.

Key terms

Socio-economic group　A group's place within society; depends on a number of factors, including occupation, education, income, wealth and where they live.

Post-school drop-out　The reduction in participation levels in young adults after they leave full-time education.

✔ Check your understanding

1　Suggest reasons for the high percentage of ethnic minority England footballers.
2　Suggest reasons for the low participation rates of Indian women.
3　How might age affect participation?

Answers are on page 187.

▲ Friends play sport together.

A person's family and friends are a huge influence on their participation in sport and physical activity. These influences can be both positive and negative. A family can have positive effects on participation through their support of a performer. This support can be financial through paying for kit or fees for coaching. They may also provide transport for training and/or matches. The support can be simply emotional, when they watch the young performer play and cheer them on.

Many parents also act as **role models** for their children. Occasionally a lack of family support can be a negative influence on participation.

Peer groups are a big influence on individuals and therefore their possible participation in sport. Peers exert pressure on their friendship groups. There is a tendency to conform to the rest of the peer group. This is often seen in the way the peers dress and behave, but may also work positively to encourage participation in certain physical activities and negatively to discourage participation in other activities.

Key terms

Role model A person looked up to by others as an example to be copied.

Peer group A group of people of approximately the same age, status and interests.

Disability participation

A person with a **disability** has some form of impairment, which affects their ability to take part in an activity.

▲ Disability is not a barrier to sports participation.

There is a wide range of conditions that come under the term disability, and it is easy to make general assumptions about those with a disability without paying attention to their specific needs, to allow disabled people equality of opportunity.

For example, a small percentage of people have a disability that is so severe that they cannot participate in physical activity or sport. Also, people with disabilities are often stereotyped as being unable to take part in physical activity.

There are three main categories of disability:

- mobility impairments
- sensory impairments
- mental impairments.

There is also disagreement over the best way to provide opportunities for those with a disability. Is it best to get disabled performers to participate with non-disabled people? This is **integration**. Or is it better to develop **adapted sports** such as wheelchair basketball specifically for disabled people?

The benefits of integration include:

- reduced possibilities of **discrimination**
- less stereotyping
- fewer barriers.

The benefits of separate opportunities include:

- greater range of opportunities through specifically designed programmes.

It is now generally thought that integration rather than separateness is better and therefore physical education and sport continues to seek ways of integrating sport and physical recreation opportunities for those with a disability within mainstream activities.

One way that people with a disability are able to participate in sport is by either adapting a mainstream version of the sport or by designing a new sport. Changing the mainstream version of a sport for people with disabilities is known as adapted sport.

Some sports have been designed to enable people with a disability to take part. They include the following:

- Boccia – A bowls-type game, played at the Paralympics and suitable for players of all abilities.
- Goalball – An active court game for visually impaired or sighted players.

> ### ✔ Check your understanding
>
> 1 What do you understand by the term integration?
> 2 What is discrimination?
> 3 What are the three types of disability?
> 4 Suggest why integration is thought to be better than separation.
> Answers are on page 187.

Key terms

Disability A physical or mental condition that limits a person's movements, senses or activities.

Integration Involving the full participation of all people in community life, but usually referring to disabled people.

Adapted sports Competitive sports for individuals with disabilities. While they often parallel existing sports played by able-bodied athletes, there may be some modifications in the equipment and rules to meet the needs of the participants.

Discrimination The unjust or prejudicial treatment of different groups of people, especially on the grounds of race, age or sex.

PRACTICE QUESTION

The participation of women in physical activities is often dependent upon the opportunities available to them. Explain the term *discrimination*.   (2 marks)

Answer is on page 188.

PRACTICE QUESTION

What is meant by the terms stereotyping and inclusiveness?   (2 marks)

Answer is on page 188.

Activity

Use the internet to research the events at the 2016 Paralympics. From that list identify six adapted sports.

Answer is on page 188.

▲ Boccia at the 2012 Paralympics.

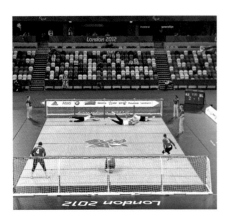
▲ Goalball at the 2012 Paralympics.

Barriers to participation

A range of barriers to participation has been identified:

- attitudes
- role models
- accessibility – to facilities/clubs/activities
- media coverage
- sexism/stereotyping
- culture/religion/religious festivals
- family commitments
- available leisure time
- familiarity
- education
- socio-economic factors/disposable income
- adaptability/inclusiveness.

A barrier to participation is an obstacle that prevents a group within society from participating in sport or physical recreation and therefore reduces overall levels of participation.

An attitude is an opinion about something and means that people have a tendency to respond in a certain way towards something. These attitudes are generally learned from family and friends. Attitudes can be positive or negative. A person may have a negative attitude about exercise and therefore does not participate; whereas another person may have a positive attitude about exercise and does take part.

Attitudes are long lasting, but they can be changed. If we want more people to participate in sport and physical activity we may need to change their negative attitude to a positive one. Attitudes can be changed by convincing the performer of all the good things about an activity, such as explaining the health benefits of exercise. They may also be changed by getting the performer to take part in the activity and finding out that they actually enjoy it, rather than hating it as they expected.

Attitudes to participation do change. The idea of women playing rugby or cricket attracted negative attitudes from most people 30 years ago, but now that general idea has changed; similarly with women's football. After the England women's success in winning the bronze medal at the 2015 World Cup, attitudes towards women's football have become much more positive.

Role models have a great influence on attitudes and participation in general. Role models can be from a sport, from family, or from a peer group. Role models tend to encourage participation in sport. They may also encourage people to play in a certain way and even influence fashion choices both on and off the field.

Knowledge of the possibility of being a role model can also influence the behaviour of the role model.

A very important factor in terms of whether a person participates in a physical activity is **accessibility**. Many physical activities require a certain type of facility in order to participate. For example, skiing needs snow or an artificial surface; disabled swimmers may need a hoist to enter and leave the water. If that facility is not easily available, then participation becomes difficult.

Some activities are only available in certain locations. Clubs, and therefore opportunities to participate, are quite difficult to locate in some parts of the country. White water canoeing needs access to the type of water found in fast-flowing rivers usually found in rural areas; it is much less accessible in cities.

Some activities are not accessible because of the cost or difficulty of transport. There are very few Olympic-size swimming pools in this country, making it difficult if you live a long distance from one of them. Many elite sportspeople have to go and live near a facility to make access to the facility easier.

Media coverage usually has a positive effect on participation in that it often generates role models or simply general interest that encourages participation. A lack of media coverage, or bad media coverage, however, can have a negative effect on participation.

The table below compares the potential positive and negative effects of media coverage.

▲ Different forms of media.

POSITIVE	NEGATIVE
Attendances may rise as people want to see the best players/role models	Attendances may fall as more people watch from home
Supporters become better informed	Only few sports on TV; minor sports not shown
Easier to attract sponsorship	Sports personalities lose privacy
Encourages participation	Events can be sensationalised to promote the media rather than the sport
Develops personalities and role models	Changes to playing season, e.g. summer rugby league
Multiple cameras give viewers a close-up view of the action	Changes to event timings, e.g. Premier League matches on Friday and Monday nights
	Changes to the rules, e.g. new scoring system for badminton

✔ Check your understanding

1 What are attitudes?
2 Identify four different forms of media.
3 Describe four negative effects that the media may have on sport.
Answers are on page 187.

Sexism is the belief that one sex (usually the male) is naturally superior to the other. It involves and leads to prejudice, stereotyping or discrimination, typically against women, on the basis of gender.

Elite sport is sexist in that it separates men and women. The men's decathlon has been an Olympic event since 1912 but there is no place for the women's event. While men play five sets at tennis Grand Slam events, women can only compete over three sets.

In terms of participation, 1.9 million fewer women than men participate in sport at least once a month. Women make up only 18 per cent of qualified coaches and 9 per cent of senior coaches. Less than 1 per cent of sports sponsorship in the UK goes to women's sport and men generally get more prize money than women. Finally, only 7 per cent of all sports media coverage in the UK is dedicated to women's events.

Activity

Use the internet to find the eventual final position of the England teams in these events and complete the following table to show the relative success of women's sports:

Event	Women	Men
Football World Cup	2015 –	2014 –
Rugby World Cup	2014 –	2015 –
Cricket World Cup	2013 –	2015 –

Answers are on page 189.

But sport is not isolated from society. The feminist movement has made great advances towards equality for women and most of these inequalities are being challenged.

There are certain groups of women affected by these issues more than others; for example, teenage girls (15–19) participate less as they grow older. The major reasons for the decline in participation by teenage girls are based on the lack of interest in physical activity from their friends and family, concerns over their weight and appearance and associated feelings of lack of confidence.

Muslim women participate less than women from other social or cultural groups. Not only does this cultural group face the same inequalities as other women, but they also have the additional cultural difficulties of needing to follow a strict dress code and the need to only mix with other women.

Key terms

Prejudice Preconceived opinion that is not based on reason or actual experience.

This is just an example of how culture and/or religion may affect participation. Other influences on the participation of ethnic minority groups include the effects of discrimination as a result of **prejudice**, which may lead to reduced opportunities either through limited access or by individuals choosing not to participate.

Another reason for lower participation rates is that a higher percentage of ethnic minority communities are in economically deprived areas and have lower disposable incomes, and therefore cannot afford to participate. Certain cultural groups may not see sports participation as a worthwhile use of time, and may place greater emphasis on academic success. There may be a need for a cultural group to observe their religious festivals, which may limit participation at certain times of the year.

Another factor is **family commitments**. Individuals may need to look after other members of their family and this may limit opportunities to participate in sport and physical activities.

▲ Family participation.

Leisure time is the time people have when they are not working, taking care of themselves or completing their family and home duties. In general, the amount of leisure time has increased in recent years for most people because they tend to now have shorter working days and shorter working careers. Linked to this is the fact that people now tend to live longer.

People also have better/easier working conditions; work tends to be less arduous and the number of paid holidays has increased. More and more people are job-sharing and involved in part-time rather than full-time work. There are also many inventions that make life easier, which means that housework takes less time.

More leisure time should mean more time for sport and physical activity, but there are still many people who through choice or through necessity still have limited leisure time due to work or other commitments.

One of the main factors that influence a person's choice of physical activity is their familiarity with that activity. Most people would rather be involved with something they already know about and understand. Some of the more common ways to have familiarity with an activity is through parental influence, where children become involved in the same activity as their parents. Participating in the same activity as a role model is another example of the use of familiarity as a deciding factor.

The activities chosen for participation are not always a person's own choice, quite often the choice is made for you. This is certainly the case in terms of the influence of education on participation. Compulsory physical education lessons give every child an introduction to activities that they may continue to participate in after leaving school.

▲ School sport.

Many factors affect a school's PE programme. Some schools simply have better and/or newer facilities than others. Many schools have PE teachers who have interests in certain sports that they emphasise in their PE lessons, but this in turn may actually limit a child's experience to certain activities. In much the same way, a school may have a tradition in a certain area – a 'rugby-playing school', for example.

In many schools the timetable can be a problem, as there may be a greater emphasis, and more lessons, given to academic subjects, and so there is insufficient time allocated to PE. Facilities and/or finance can also affect PE provision. For example, without a pool, a school may find it very expensive to provide swimming lessons for its pupils. A similar restriction occurs with outdoor and adventure activities, which are expensive to organise, especially when travel and accommodation become part of the cost.

As previously mentioned, socio-economic factors have a big influence on participation in physical activity. Surveys have shown that individuals from lower socio-economic groups are less likely to participate in physical activity.

The main reason for this lower level of participation by certain socio-economic groups is because of the lower **disposable income** available to spend on leisure activities. In much the same way, people from lower socio-economic groups may have limited leisure time because of the need to work long hours. But also, some activities are associated with certain social groups, leading to possible rejection or discrimination, and some activities still have membership that is restricted to certain socio-economic groups. For example, there is a need to own a pony, which is expensive, in order to participate in polo.

Finally, one way that people with limited access to an activity, such as those with a disability or with limited disposable income are able to participate in sport is by either adapting a mainstream version of the sport or by designing a new sport. This makes many activities inclusive to all. For example, the sport of basketball can be adapted to wheelchair basketball for disabled users. The sport of polo can be adapted to bicycle polo for people with limited disposable income. Adapting an activity to enable more people to participate is making an activity **inclusive**.

PRACTICE QUESTION

Suggest reasons for the lower participation rates for people with a disability. (4 marks)

Answer is on page 188.

Study hint

The majority of the factors affecting participation affect most social groups. Learn the groups and how each factor could affect participation.

Rapid recall

Use the acronym **T I M E** to help remember factors affecting participation.

T = **t**ime (lack of); **I** = **i**ncome (lack of);
M = **m**obility (no transport);
E = **e**ducation (awareness of benefits)

Activity

Make a list of the factors that could affect the participation of women in physical activity and sport.

Answer is on page 189.

Key terms

Leisure time The time we have when we are not working, taking care of ourselves or completing our family and home duties. It has increased as a result of shorter working careers and increased life expectancy.

Disposable income Income available to be spent or saved as one wishes.

Inclusive Including everybody.

✔ Check your understanding

1 Suggest four factors that affect participation of disabled people.
2 Suggest four different factors that affect participation of women.
3 Suggest four reasons why women's participation numbers are increasing.
Answers are on page 187.

Summary

- Engagement patterns differ between different social groups
- There is a variety of factors that affect engagement patterns of different social groups

Chapter 5b Commercialisation of physical activity and sport

Chapter objectives

- Understand the idea of commercialisation and the relationship between sport, sponsorship and the media
- Understand the positive and negative impacts of sponsorship and the media
- Understand the positive and negative impacts of technology

Commercialisation

Commercialisation is the process of introducing a new product into commerce – the activity of buying and selling, especially on a large scale. Sports and sports performers are products that can be bought or sold. Teams can buy and sell players, sports can sell competitions, media can buy and sell sports, businesses can buy and sell sports. Businesses can buy and sell competitions, grounds, teams and players. Sports, grounds, competitions, teams and players can advertise businesses.

Every aspect of sport has now become a commodity that can be bought and sold. Virtually all professional sports teams and sports organisations employ a marketing manager whose job is to sell the sport/team to anybody willing to buy part of that team/sport.

In today's society, sport is inextricably linked to the media and to **sponsorship** in what is known as the **golden triangle**.

Key terms

Commercialisation The process by which a new product or service is introduced into the general market.

Media The main ways that people communicate (television, radio, and newspapers) collectively.

Sponsorship Where a company pays money to a team or individual in return for advertising their goods.

Golden triangle The financial relationship between sport, sponsorship and media.

> ### Activity
>
> Watch the YouTube clip on the golden triangle at: 'A sponsorship triangle: Sports, media and corporations'
>
> https://www.youtube.com/watch?v=n1i8GzkcFMM

▲ The golden triangle.

The media includes things such as radio, newspapers, magazines, books and the internet, but the major impact is through television.

Sports are watched by **spectators**, either live at the event or at home on TV.

▲ An example of sponsorship in sport.

Key terms

Spectators People who watch sport; can be at the event or watch/listening/reading – 'armchair spectating'.

Philanthropic Trying to benefit others; generous.

Sponsorship is the idea of a company providing resources in return for some business-related favour/advantage. Sponsorship is simply a form of advertising to increase sales of a product and/or make the company's name more well known.

In this relationship, the sport is sold to businesses as a means of advertising the business's product. The business sponsors the sport to obtain advertising space and publicise its product. The sport is shown on the media, which promotes the product, and the sport spectators see the advertising and buy the business's product.

Commercialised sport is driven by the need to make a profit for the people involved, and the need for success. This may lead to a change in attitude by the people involved because of the need to win to make money. Performers are forced to promote the sport to sell the sponsor's product being advertised.

Sport has become much more professionally managed. Teams and sports are now run and organised by people with a background in business. This is because in order to make money, a sport (or team) must attract sponsors, but sponsors are only interested if the sport gets good media coverage that will advertise the sponsor's product.

Sponsorship

Sponsorship appears to be a great benefit to sport. In fact, without sponsorship, sport as we know it would have to change, because of all the money involved. Businesses sponsor sport mainly as a means of advertising their product. If the sponsored sport is regularly in the media then spectators will see the sponsor's name and this publicity may increase sales of the product.

Many businesses sponsor a sport in order to associate the name of the product with a successful or popular team or individual. The thought they are hoping to get into the spectator's head is that if this team is quality then the sponsor's product must be quality. The sponsor wants the spectator to buy its product.

There are sponsors whose main aim is not so much to gain increased sales of its product, but rather to support the local community. Local businesses will often support local sports teams simply with the intention of helping others. This is almost a form of charity and is said to be **philanthropic**.

What does the sponsor get out of this? Money used by a business for sponsorship is tax deductible; in other words, part of what is spent by a sponsor is regained by getting a lower tax bill.

The sponsor is not always providing money; other forms of support such as company products are more usually provided. Sponsors may provide items such as equipment, clothing or footwear. Similarly, the sponsorship is not always to a sport; businesses can sponsor an individual, a team, a competition, a stadium or a stand.

There are negatives to sponsoring a sport. The sponsor's name becomes linked to the activity, which is good provided that the activity is seen in a positive light by the spectators. But, being linked to an activity that is performing badly reflects badly on the sponsor. Similarly, any negative aspects to a sport, such as cheating, violence or bad results reflect negatively on the sponsor's product.

▲ Sponsorship advertises the sponsor's name.

Sport and the media

Sport is a fairly cheap form of entertainment for TV companies; it costs less to show a sporting event than a drama production or a soap. It also has most of the requirements of a 'good' programme – lots of excitement and only a few periods when the action slows.

In order to publicise itself, a sport must be attractive to the media. This has led to some sports changing to make themselves more attractive to the spectator. In 'good to watch' sports, there are short bursts of maximum excitement, e.g. 100 m sprint or a goal in football.

There have even been examples of the creation of new forms of a sport simply because they were more attractive to a TV audience, e.g. 20/20 cricket.

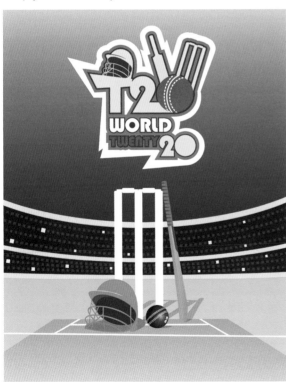

▲ New forms of sport invented for TV.

Activity

Choose a sport and research it on the internet. Make a list of various sponsors linked to that sport. For each sponsor, try to suggest the main reason for their sponsorship.

✔ Check your understanding

1 What is commercialised sport?
2 What are the three parts of the golden triangle?
3 What is sponsorship?
4 State three benefits of sponsorship to the sponsor.

Answers are on page 189.

Rapid recall

Reasons for sponsoring form the acronym **PAST** – **P**ublicity, **A**ssociation, **S**upport, **T**ax.

Many aspects of popular sports have been changed for TV. Kick-off times at the World Cup (and other competitions) are scheduled to attract a maximum viewing audience. Football has its biggest TV audience in Europe, so wherever the finals are held, the European teams involved will kick off at a time that presents them playing at about 8 p.m. in Europe, when maximum viewing figures can be guaranteed.

In terms of media, television is viewed as the 'best' form of media for sport, because it provides images that can be transmitted live. Television, radio and newspapers are all easy to access but television, because it is live, may sometimes be unable to provide as much in-depth information as radio and newspapers.

Satellite and cable television (SKY and BTSport) exist as competition to the traditional terrestrial channels (BBC and ITV). This competition is essentially based on sport, with football having the highest viewing figures for all satellite programmes.

Sport can also be easily left for a few minutes without the viewer losing the plot. Sports coverage has also benefited from developments in technology, with 'action replays' leading the way.

The media requires sport to fit into its needs. Sport that is good for television has the following characteristics:

- It demonstrates skill, strength and physical fitness.
- It is competitive and spectacular with detail available.
- It has simple rule structures.
- It fits into a reasonable time scale.
- Personalities are easily identified.
- It is easy to televise, e.g. cameras able to keep up with play, reasonable-sized playing area.

Activity

Choose one individual sport and one team sport and list examples of how they fit into the idea of what is required for 'good' television.

Radio readily provides information about sport and can do so in great detail. Radio programmes can provide commentaries from sports events. These are intended to 'paint a picture' for the listener. Similarly, radio often provides in-depth interviews, with performers or experts in sports providing information.

Both radio and television can be 'live', whereas newspapers and **social media** are delayed to a certain extent. The internet can be both live and delayed.

Newspapers tend to appear in one of two forms – broadsheet or tabloid – although some broadsheets are now appearing in tablet versions. Both types have to sell large numbers of newspapers to make a profit. To sell copies, the two different types adopt different ways to attract readers.

▲ There are different types of newspapers.

Broadsheet newspapers tend to emphasise themselves as an information service; they have less of the total paper devoted to sport, but a more varied coverage in terms of a wider range of sports. The broadsheets also tend to provide critical analysis of events and issues affecting sport.

The tabloid newspapers tend to sensationalise events and personalities. They tend to focus on a narrow range of popular sports – e.g. football, horse racing – and having little coverage of minority sports. Most tabloids have a larger proportion of the total (up to a quarter) newspaper devoted to sport.

The internet and social media are fast becoming the major forms of media in sport. The internet is now regularly used for sport coverage, allowing people to obtain the latest news about their favourite team, sport or event. The methods that are available for delivering sport to different sections of society continue to grow rapidly.

It has been said that the new media explosion makes 'any sport, any event, any time, any device' a reality for the fan. The list of possible outlets for sport is ever increasing: high definition and 3D television, Internet Protocol TV, mobile phones, YouTube, web streaming, digital radio, iPlayer, games consoles and social networking sites.

Originally the internet was mostly a one-way experience. People visited a website to read the content but had limited ways to interact. Access was by a computer. More recently, the internet has become more social. People can interact, generate and share multi-media content across the web. Websites have become interactive in terms of content and are accessible from multiple devices – computers, mobile phones, interactive TV, media players and games consoles.

Social media are media for social interaction. Social media use web-based technologies to turn communication into interactive discussions. Social media is all about sharing rather than discovering information.

Spectators are using social media channels not only to take in information but also to create information and interact with other users. Facebook, Twitter, LinkedIn, Digg, Instagram, Blogspot, WordPress and Flickr are examples of popular social networking channels that sports fans can use to interact with their teams, individuals or businesses related to their teams.

Activity

Obtain a broadsheet and a tabloid newspaper (this could be done as a classroom activity). Calculate how many 'column inches' are used for each sport in each newspaper. Draw a graph to show your results.

Key term

Social media Websites and applications that allow users to create and share content.

▲ Social media.

Key term

Marketability Able to be sold.

Activity

Read newspaper articles at:
'How sport dominated social media in 2014'

http://www.theguardian.com/football/2014/dec/10/how-sport-dominated-social-media-in-2014

and

'The importance of social media in sport'

http://www.telegraph.co.uk/sponsored/business/business-sport-series/11691416/social-media-in-sport.html

PRACTICE QUESTION

What are the disadvantages to a sport of increased media control?   (4 marks)

Answers are on page 190.

✔ **Check your understanding**

1 List five forms of media.
2 How do radio and newspapers try to compete with TV?
3 What are the two main types of newspaper?

Answers are on page 189.

Commercialised activity and the performer

The media often focus on individual personalities rather than the event. Therefore, performers have to be aware of the need to entertain in order to increase their **marketability**.

The high income of many elite performers and the lifestyle it offers restricts the performer's ability to move in 'normal' society, especially with the amount of media intrusion into their social background.

Sponsorship usually means that the team or individual performances improve because the additional income gives them more time to train, better venues to train in and better equipment to use – all of which should mean that skills and fitness develop.

The performer may get free equipment, clothing or footwear. They may even be paid for wearing that clothing and using that equipment. The performer will be under less stress to win because of the reduced worry about finances.

However, there are some negative aspects. The contract between the sponsors and the performer may demand that the performer has to submit to various commitments such as meeting corporate hosts and talking to the media, which may mean a loss of free time or privacy.

The sponsor's product may not be entirely suitable in terms of the performer's values, such as being thought of as unhealthy. A run of poor results may lead to a loss of sponsorship and therefore income. Such a trend could lead to a performer looking to cheat to prevent such a run and maintain their sponsorship.

Commercialised activity and the sport

Sponsorship has increased the income for many sports, so they do not have to rely on income from spectators. Sponsorship has provided the finances for the development of new competitions and has provided increased media interest.

But not all sponsorship is good. Sponsorship relies on the media. The media concentrate on 'the best', often to the detriment of the 'not quite the best'. So the big sports, for example football in the UK, get the big money, and minor sports get very little.

For example, the broadcasting rights to Premier League football, bought by Sky and BT Sport for the three years from the 2016/17 season to the end of the 2019/20 season were worth over £5 billion. That means an average price of £10 million for the teams when their game is shown live. This is the same amount as the annual sponsorship being given to UK Athletics by Sainsbury's.

Sponsors, because they are putting so much money into sport, are gaining more and more control over sport in terms of what is shown on TV, when it's shown and who is shown. For example, the images that are shown on TV are invariably arranged to show the sponsor's name. The sponsor decides where to place the sponsor's name and logo, and where to place the cameras in order to get the sponsor's name maximum exposure and maximum publicity.

Activity

Read the newspaper article at:

'Premier League TV rights: Sky and BT pay £5.1 bn for live games'

http://www.bbc.co.uk/sport/0/football/31357409

▲ On-pitch advertising.

The timings of events are now determined by the sponsors to maximise the potential for publicity. Premiership football, again, is the best example. Matches are staged at different times over different days of the weekend to maximise the number of spectators.

Teams change their strips to suit their sponsors. Most sponsorship deals last two or three years and each new deal will involve several new kits.

Activity

Research and make a list of how many different sports are on television (all channels) in any three-day period. What are the five main televised sports?

Effects of commercialisation on officials

Commercialisation of sport is all about money. The money brings its own benefits and problems for officials.

Officials can get paid to officiate, and their income has increased in recent years. People who officiate elite sport are invariably full-time; officiating is their job. In most elite sports, if matches are being played more frequently, then more matches can be officiated by the relative few high-calibre officials.

A top football or rugby union referee can earn £50,000–£100,000 p.a. Matches are held around the world, so there is the opportunity to travel. Many officials can become nearly as famous as the players they control.

▲ Mark Clattenburg, football referee.

But there are downsides, mainly because of the media coverage involved. Officials are regularly placed in the media spotlight over decisions they have made. Making a bad decision can lead to being dropped from the elite panel of officials and, with social media, severe criticism from the general public.

The modern-day official has to be prepared to take the rough with the smooth in much the same way as the professional sportsperson in terms of accusations of not performing well, being biased, cheating, etc.

> ### ✅ Check your understanding
>
> 1 List four ways that sponsors can support an individual other than supplying money.
> 2 State three possible disadvantages of sponsorship to an individual.
> 3 Suggest three ways that sponsors can influence a sport.
> 4 Suggest two benefits and two disadvantages of commercialisation for officials.
>
> Answers are on page 189.

Effects of commercialisation on spectators

In general, commercialisation has been beneficial for spectators. There is more money available for better players to be brought in and matches are played at a higher standard. Facilities have improved for spectating at the match, with many teams updating existing facilities or moving to new improved facilities.

▲ Manchester City's new Etihad Stadium.

The spectators can be more involved through the use of huge TV screens to show replays, statistics and other information, which also makes them more informed and knowledgeable about the activity. The spectators can associate themselves more clearly with the activity through buying merchandise.

▲ TV screens provide information for spectators.

Changing the format of a sport, together with longer seasons, means that there are more opportunities for spectators to watch their favourite sport.

The armchair spectator can see many more games using a wide range of different camera angles. There are more sports available to watch than ever before with dedicated sports channels on TV, radio and websites. There are also sport-specific newspapers.

The main problem for the armchair spectator is the isolation from the live match, but TV tends to compensate for that through the use of crowd noise, specialist camera positions, the use of the red button to offer a preferred view and informed opinion from 'experts'.

Effects of commercialisation on sponsors

Commercialisation provides sponsors with the publicity they require for their product. The advertising through sport attracts a very large audience and many people will want to be associated with sporting success. The status of the product is linked to that success. There could be increased sales of the product and therefore increased income for the business.

On the negative side, anything that occurs in a sport that is harmful to that sport, team or individual will also affect the sponsor and potentially the sales of the product. So things such as crowd trouble, a run of poor results, cheating or drug taking may affect the reputation of the sponsor.

PRACTICE QUESTIONS

In what ways has an increase in the 'commercialisation' of sport been beneficial for performers and the sport?

(4 marks)

Answer is on page 190.

✔ Check your understanding

1 List three benefits to spectators of commercialisation.
2 List two disadvantages of commercialisation for spectators.
3 Describe a sporting situation that would be perfect for a sponsor.

Answers are on page 189.

Activity

'How technology is affecting sports'

Read more at:
http://www.
sportsnetworker.com/
2010/05/12/how-technology-
is-affecting-sports/

Key terms

Technology A method that is developed to try to improve performance.

Hawkeye An optical ball-tracking device used as an aid to officiating in tennis and cricket.

Television Match Official (TMO) Used in rugby union and rugby league to make decisions using replays of incidents.

Key terms

Ice-baths Used to reduce temperature in muscles after activity to speed up recovery.

Oxygen (hypoxic) tents Tents that contain high oxygen concentrations to speed up recovery after injury.

Hyperbaric chambers High pressure chambers that force oxygen into an injury to speed up recovery.

Technological developments in sport

Sport has changed over the years, and the use of more and more **technology** has made an impact on many modern-day sports. If it wasn't for technology there would be no instant replays, third umpires, or even microphones for referees to communicate with their assistants.

In other words, technology is used by performers, coaches and officials to try to improve performance; it is used to improve the experience of spectators; it can be used to improve a sport.

One criticism of the use of technology is that it can slow down the speed of the game, but on the other hand, for many people, it makes watching sport more enjoyable as they can see the correct decisions being made. For example, technology such as '**Hawkeye**' in cricket and tennis or the '**Television Match Official**' (TMO) in cricket and rugby are both used by the officials to make sure their decisions are correct, and have now become part of the sports' spectator appeal.

▲ Hawkeye is used in tennis for line calls.

Positive and negative impacts of technology on the performer

For the performer, recent developments in sporting technologies have created a variety of products aimed at improving performance. The health and well-being of performers can be maintained and observed, and injuries treated, through the production of technologies such as heart-rate monitors, pedometers and body-fat monitors.

Nutrition and fitness are probably the most important factors which can affect an athlete's performance in sport. Technology such as software programmes are being used to monitor and analyse an athlete's nutrition and fitness levels in much more accurate ways than previously.

Technology in the form of computer software and 'calorie counters' means that diets are now manipulated so that athletes reach peak nutrition for their event.

This type of technology has given individuals greater knowledge of the body's ability to absorb repeated exercise, which in turn has allowed performers to train and become much fitter, resulting in better performances.

The safety of those involved has also been increased through the development of certain sporting equipment, such as the helmets and body protection used in cricket and hockey to help prevent injuries.

Rehabilitation from injuries is now much quicker because of advances in technology through the use of **ice-baths**, **oxygen (hypoxic) tents** and **hyperbaric chambers**.

Sports equipment such as clothing and footwear needs to be user-friendly and includes valuable properties such as strength, flexibility, toughness, resistance to moisture and, more importantly, has cost advantages.

Clothing such as the full-body suits used in cycling, where winning or losing is measured in hundredths of a second, has become increasingly used. Sporting equipment such as the composite tennis racket has been created in order to provide increased ball speed and reduce the potential for overuse injuries on the elbow.

Prosthetics have also been made for athletes with a specific disability. Examples include those worn by those athletes without a lower limb, which act with a 'springboard' effect, to help the performer run.

All performances are now studied in detail through DVD recordings and developing computer software leads to detailed **match analysis**. The analysis can tell a coach when a player is beginning to lose fitness so they may be substituted. It can also be used to analyse opponents' weaknesses and enable tactical adjustments to be made.

The negatives to the use of technology for the performer are generally based around cost. As technology develops so the performer needs to keep up to date, and buy and use the latest technology in order to gain that slight advantage that separates the winner from the loser.

Technology also means that the performer is never alone. In much the same way as a performance can be analysed for weaknesses so that it can be improved, it can also be analysed by the opposition to highlight those weaknesses, or to copy all the good aspects.

Increased use of technology to improve performance could lead to the increased chance of injury and the possibility of shorter careers for the performers. Developments in technology could also lead to more cheating; for example, new performance-enhancing drugs being developed and used by performers. Similarly, the attempt to improve though the use of technology could lead to cheating through the use of electric motors being fitted inside racing bikes to improve performance.

> ### ✔ Check your understanding
>
> 1 State one benefit and one disadvantage of using Hawkeye.
> 2 List four benefits of technology to performers.
> 3 List two disadvantages to the spectator of technology.
>
> Answers are on page 189.

Positive and negative impacts of technology on sport

Technology has changed sport. For example, judgements are made not based on the human eye or an official's instinct, but rather through electronic timing, photo-finish cameras, instant replays, third umpires and technologies such as Hawkeye.

Activity

Read the article at:
'Mile-high club: do oxygen tents boost athletic performance?'
http://www.wired.com/2009/07/mile-high-club-can-oxygen-tents-boost-athletic-performance/

▲ Prosthetic limbs for disabled performers.

Key terms

Prosthetics Artificial aid; often replacing a limb.

Match analysis Computer software that provides detailed statistical data about individual and/or team performances.

Sports must appeal to the technology and, if necessary, change to accommodate technology. Advances in technology have had a deep impact on sport including:

- analysis of sport performance has allowed coaches to greatly improve the quality of feedback given to performers
- increased accuracy in time and distance measurements of performance
- referees, umpires and other officials are enabled to make better decisions on rule infringements
- improved design of sport equipment, clothing and footwear
- providing spectators with better viewing of sport.

But technology has also had its disadvantages in that sports are now not often undertaken on an equal basis. Those with access to the best technology are often the winners. Also, the time taken waiting for off-field decisions is often frustrating for spectators.

Positive and negative impacts of technology on officials

Technology is available for officials to use to make correct decisions. In most team sports, the various officials are able to communicate with each other through microphones and headsets.

In sports such as tennis and cricket, technology such as Hawkeye, which is essentially a ball-tracking software, is used to ensure officials' decisions are accurate.

A similar situation occurs in rugby union and rugby league, where another, off-field official is able to make decisions based on multiple camera angles.

These delays in making decisions are thought by some to slow the game down, but for many the waiting creates excitement. Such technology also provides coaches and/or players with the benefit of 'appealing' a decision, which is not normally available.

The technology available to officials means that some of the pressure or criticism levelled at them is reduced because decisions are made with the benefit of the technology, rather than instantaneously.

Unfortunately, the technology can never be perfect and decisions are still made that some feel are wrong. There is also the danger that officials become over-reliant on technology and slow the game down too much while making a decision. In doing so it changes the nature of the sport, which is probably why football has yet to make full use of technology in deciding things such as offside or penalties – the wait for a decision would change the game too much.

Another problem with technology is the cost. Not all sports/teams/individuals can afford the latest technology.

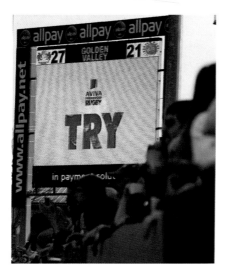

▲ A Television Match Official decision.

Positive and negative impacts of technology on spectators

Technological developments mean that spectators have an increased experience at home through the use of more cameras. There is a wider range of sports accessible through technology; for example, using glass walls and a reflective ball in squash.

The use of all-weather surfaces has led to improved skills from the performer because of the truer bounce. These surfaces have also meant that more matches can be played without damaging the surface.

Spectators now have the benefit of improved camera technology; for example, use of the red button, Hawkeye, player cams, post/stump cameras.

Spectators are also now much better informed about the activity through the on-screen information that can be supplied; for example, number of shots on target. This makes the sport much more interactive for the spectator.

▲ Television's red button.

Positive and negative impacts of technology on sponsors

Technology has assisted sponsors in how they are able to advertise their products. More cameras mean more chance of the sponsor's logo being seen. Logos are often painted onto the pitch to advertise sponsors. In some sports, especially in the USA, camera technology means that logos can be shown on-screen without being present on the pitch.

More advertising usually leads to more sales and more profit, which is usually what the sponsor intended.

However, the negative effects of technology such as injuries, cheating and losing can also negatively affect the sponsors through their links with the performer/sport.

PRACTICE QUESTION

Suggest how the increased use of technology has helped officials to make the correct decision. (3 marks)

Answer is on page 190.

✔ Check your understanding

1 State three benefits of technology to a sport.
2 Suggest why football does not use a TMO.
3 State three benefits of technology to sponsors.

Answers are on pages 189–190.

Summary

- There is a clear relationship – the golden triangle – between sport, sponsorship and the media; each now relies heavily on the other
- There are both positive and negative impacts of commercialisation on those involved in sport
- Technology is having an ever-increasing influence, both positive and negative on those involved in sport

Chapter objectives

- Understand how the conduct of performers may vary
- Understand the different prohibited substances and the methods that certain types of performers may use
- Understand the positive and the negative effects of spectators at events

Players' conduct

The way people play sports is fixed by the rules, but there are also unwritten rules which people try to abide by whether they are playing or spectating. These rules are about behaviour and are known as **etiquette**.

▲ Etiquette.

For example, in football, players usually kick the ball out of play if another player is injured so that they can get treatment. The team that kicked the ball out then get the ball back when the opposition throw it to them when play restarts. In many games, players shake their opponents' hands and those of the officials after the match. In some sports, such as golf, players are expected to officiate themselves and even own up to breaking the rules.

These are examples of **sportsmanship**; sometimes called fair play. Sportsmanship is playing fair, showing respect for the opposition, and gracious behaviour in winning or losing. On the other hand, **gamesmanship** is coming close to breaking the rules, without getting punished. For example, time wasting when you are winning is not against the rules, but is probably not fair play. In tennis, players sometimes try to break their opponent's concentration by re-tying their shoe laces when an important serve is about to happen.

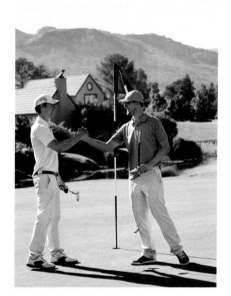

▲ Sportsmanship.

Key terms

Etiquette The unwritten rules concerning player behaviour.

Sportsmanship Appropriate, polite and fair behaviour while participating in a sporting event.

Gamesmanship The use of dubious methods, that are not strictly illegal, to gain an advantage.

▲ Diving is not gamesmanship; it is cheating.

The **contract to compete** is linked to the idea of sportsmanship and is the agreement that in sport players try to win, play within the rules and etiquette and allow the opposition a free and fair opportunity to win. The contract to compete is usually in the performer's head rather than written down. It is occasionally seen to be agreed; for example, when players shake hands before a football match. The contract to compete is trying your hardest and allowing the opposition to play.

✔ Check your understanding

1 What is etiquette?
2 Give three examples of sportsmanship from a team game.
3 What is gamesmanship?
4 What is the contract to compete?

Answers are on pages 190–191.

Prohibited substances

There are a large number of products which may be taken to help sports performance in some way. These are known as **ergogenic aids** or performance enhancing drugs (PEDs). PEDs are banned by **National Governing Bodies** of sport and the **International Olympic Committee**.

> **Activity**
>
> Read the following article:
>
> 'Rugby tops list of drug-test failures'
>
> http://www.telegraph.co.uk/sport/othersports/drugsinsport/2297419/Rugby-tops-list-of-drug-test-failures.html

PRACTICE QUESTION

Is diving in football gamesmanship or bad sportsmanship? Explain your answer.   (3 marks)

Answer is on page 191.

PRACTICE QUESTION

How is the ethic of sportsmanship encouraged and maintained at the highest level of sport?   (2 marks)

Answer is on page 191.

▲ Shaking hands before a match means 'we agree to the contract to compete'.

Key terms

Contract to compete Agreeing to play by the rules, trying to win but also allowing your opponent to play.

National Governing Body Organisation with responsibility for managing their specific sport.

International Olympic Committee The independent authority of the worldwide modern Olympic movement. It organises the Olympic Games.

Ergogenic aid A technique or substance used for the purpose of enhancing performance.

▲ Drugs can improve performance.

Key terms

Adrenaline Naturally occurring hormone that prepares the body for 'fight or flight'.

Stimulants Make athletes more alert and mask effects of fatigue.

Narcotic analgesics Painkillers that mask pain caused by injury or fatigue, which can make the injury worse.

Anabolic agents Drugs that help athletes to train harder and build muscle.

Peptide hormones (EPO) Naturally occurring chemicals. EPO increases numbers of red blood cells and therefore improves oxygen delivery to muscles.

Stimulants

Stimulants are substances that speed up parts of the brain and body. **Adrenaline** is an example of a naturally occurring stimulant in the body. Some athletes may use stimulants in an attempt to increase alertness, reduce reaction time, reduce tiredness and increase their aggressiveness.

Examples of stimulants are amphetamines and caffeine. They are highly addictive and have side effects including high blood pressure, strokes and heart and liver problems. They can also increase the risk of injury because the performer is more tolerant to pain and will continue to train or compete with an injury.

Performers who are injured and want to return to competition or full-time training may be tempted to use stimulants to deaden pain. The most likely users, however, would be those performers who need to be more alert, such as sprinters and speed swimmers who need a fast reaction time at the start of a race.

Narcotic analgesics

Narcotic analgesics are very strong painkillers which performers could use to mask pain from an injury or overtraining. They are highly addictive and cause withdrawal symptoms when you stop using them.

Examples of narcotic analgesics include heroin and morphine. Constipation and low blood pressure are side effects, as is loss of concentration leading to possible coma. Performers who need to recover from excessive overtraining or compete with an injury may be tempted to use these.

Anabolic agents

Athletes may use anabolic agents to increase the rate and amount of muscle growth. The most common type is the anabolic steroid. These also speed up recovery so performers are able to train harder and more frequently. Common examples include Nandrolone and Danazol.

Performers take anabolic agents to build up body weight and to increase the size of muscles and therefore their strength. These drugs may also make the user more aggressive and competitive. Like many other banned substances they are also addictive.

Heavy, regular use of anabolic agents can shrink the testicles in men, cause high blood pressure and damage the liver, kidneys and heart. Women may develop more body hair, smaller breasts and a deeper voice.

Peptide hormones (EPO)

These are naturally occurring substances that can improve muscle growth and increase production of red blood cells, which increases oxygen delivery to muscles.

One **peptide hormone** is **EPO** (Erythropoietin), which will increase the numbers of red blood cells in the body, and therefore increase the ability of an athlete's blood to transport oxygen to cells that are producing energy during exercise. This additional oxygen reduces the fatigue felt in muscles in long distance events such as marathon running and cycling. The side effects of EPO are caused by the thickening of the blood which requires the heart to pump harder and can lead to an increased risk of stroke or heart attack.

Diuretics

Diuretics are drugs such as Frusemide that are taken to remove excess water from the body. They are not used to improve actual performance; they are used for other reasons. First, to lose weight rapidly in sports that require the performer to be within a set weight limit; for example, boxers and jockeys. Second, to dilute the presence of illegal substances and aid their removal from the body in urine.

Diuretics cause severe **dehydration**, low blood pressure and muscle cramps, and may be taken by any performer to hide other PED use.

Blood doping

Blood doping is the use of techniques and/or substances to increase a performer's red blood cell count.

The simplest form of blood doping involves the removal of about two pints of blood from the athlete several weeks before a competition. In the time before the competition the body will make more blood to replace the amount taken out. The removed blood is frozen until 1–2 days before the competition, when it is thawed and injected back into the athlete. The use of EPO is really a form of blood doping.

Blood doping is most commonly used by endurance athletes, such as marathon runners and cyclists. By increasing the number of red blood cells, the blood can carry more oxygen to the muscles where it can be used for energy.

The following side effects can occur with blood doping:

- increased thickening of blood (**viscosity**)
- potential for heart attacks
- risk of blood-borne diseases such as HIV and hepatitis
- **embolism** (a blockage of a blood vessel).

Beta blockers

Beta blockers reduce the effects of adrenaline on the body. They reduce the heart rate and reduce muscle tension and blood pressure. By doing this, they improve a performer's fine motor control and will increase precision when doing motor skills. Beta blockers could be taken by performers who need to reduce the effects of nerves and use fine motor skills, such as players in target sports.

The side effects of beta blockers include nausea, poor circulation leading to heart problems, tiredness and weakness. Sports performers may only take beta blockers if they have been prescribed by a medical professional.

Key terms

Diuretics Drugs that remove fluid from the body.

Dehydration A condition that occurs when the body loses more water than it takes in.

Key terms

Blood doping Artificially increasing the number of red cells in the blood.

Viscosity How 'thick' a liquid is.

Embolism Blood clot.

Beta blockers Drugs taken to calm performer down by reducing the effects of adrenaline.

PRACTICE QUESTION

Taking EPO is a form of blood doping. What are the supposed benefits of this practice and what type of performer might take EPO?

(3 marks)

Answer is on page 191.

PRACTICE QUESTION

Suggest why a performer might take anabolic agents.

(2 marks)

Answer is on page 192.

Rapid recall

An acronym for reasons for drug-taking = **FILS**: **F**ame, **I**ncome, **L**evel playing field, **S**uccess.

Rapid recall

Construct an acronym for the disadvantages of taking PEDs; for example, Clear Bans For Risking Heroin? **C**heating, **B**ans, **F**ines, **R**eputation, **H**ealth risks.

Activity

Make a list of the advantages and disadvantages to the performer of taking PEDs.

Answer is on page 192.

✔ Check your understanding

1 Why might a performer use stimulants?
2 What type of performer might use anabolic agents?
3 What are the side effects of narcotic analgesic use?

Answers are on page 191.

Activity

Complete the following table:

Effects on athlete	Type of PED	Sport that might benefit
Enhance alertness	Stimulant	
Reduce heart rate		Archery
	EPO	Cycling
Mask drug use	Diuretics	
	Anabolic agents	Weight-lifting
Mask pain		Football

Answer is on page 192.

The advantages and disadvantages to the performer of taking PEDs

The reasons athletes use performance enhancing drugs is that they have a lot of benefits which allow the performer to play better, keep their careers going and keep them employed.

Athletes are under pressure to perform, and PEDs can be a way for them to keep up with the competition. Since their income depends on performance, it's not a surprise that some sportspeople may take advantage of the benefits of PEDs.

The potential advantages of PEDs are better performance and therefore an increased chance of success. As a professional performer, hand in hand with the success will come the increase in income, and linked to this will be greater recognition or fame for the performer.

One often mentioned reason for the taking of PEDs is the performer's thoughts that everybody else is taking them, so why not join in? In doing so, the performer probably thinks they are simply keeping a level playing field.

Some of these PEDs may come with associated health risks, but they also have several disadvantages that need to be considered.

First, it is cheating. It is immoral and is against the whole idea of what sport is and the concepts of sportsmanship and etiquette. Taking PEDs is against the contract to compete.

Second, as testing procedures become ever more accurate and regular, it becomes more and more likely that the cheats will be caught. Performers who test positive for banned substances usually face a two-year ban from their sport. They will also be fined. Perhaps the biggest disadvantage concerning being caught taking PEDs is the damage to the performer's reputation and the long-term negative publicity they will face.

The disadvantages to the sport of performers taking PEDs

Despite the fines, bans, health risks and damage to their reputation, some performers still take PEDs. Certain sports have lost their reputation because of the number of positive tests that have occurred. Spectators become quite cynical about exceptional performances and are inclined to think 'Was that due to drugs?' rather than 'That was an outstanding performance'. Some sports such as cycling and athletics begin to lose their credibility because of the regular positive drugs test.

Sports could lose income through reduced numbers of spectators or through loss of sponsorship. Participation levels could fall.

Spectator behaviour

The whole basis for sports is the idea of playing for fun. But as interest in sport grew, people began paying to watch, and so sports became commercialised as people paid to watch the matches/events. Paying spectators enabled various sports clubs to make a profit and use this money to develop the sport.

Some sports with large spectator bases were able to pay for better performers and so encourage an increase in spectating. These sports became professional in that they paid their players to play.

The increased interest in spectating led to increased media attention. The early media that embraced a massed audience were newspapers and the radio, but TV provided the spur to the dramatic increase in the commercialisation of sport that we now see.

The televising of sport works in two ways. First, it provides a relatively cheap form of production that can be shown live or in a highlights package. Second, it dramatically increases the number of spectators from the thousands at the event to the millions in their homes.

While spectators do not have any effect on a performer's physical ability, they can make or break some performers' concentration. Spectators don't just watch, they are actively and vocally involved in the experience. Many cheer for the team or individual they are backing and whistle or boo the opposition. This creates an atmosphere at the event.

It is commonly accepted that cheering positively influences a team's performance. When playing a match, the home team receives much more support from the crowd in attendance. This is called **home-field advantage** and explains why most teams have better results at home than when playing away.

If the atmosphere created by the loud support for the home team is an advantage, there are also negative aspects to spectating. The atmosphere itself can be intimidating, especially if a performer is not used to it. The positive effects of home-field advantage must also act as negative effects on the away team, hindering performance. The same thing could happen to the home players, with the spectators expecting a positive result and increasing the pressure to perform.

✔ Check your understanding

1 What are the effects of taking EPO?
2 What effects do diuretics have?
3 What type of performer might use blood doping?
4 What are beta blockers?

Answers are on page 191.

PRACTICE QUESTION

Some performers may take PEDs to improve performance. Suggest two potential advantages and two potential disadvantages of a performer taking drugs.

(4 marks)

Answer is on page 192.

Key terms

PED Performance Enhancing Drug.

Home-field advantage The psychological advantage that the home team has over the visiting team as a result of playing in familiar facilities and in front of supportive fans.

✔ Check your understanding

1 Suggest three possible benefits to the performer of taking PEDs.
2 Identify three disadvantages to the performer of taking PEDs.
3 List two effects on a sport that a positive drug test might have.

Answers are on page 191.

Key term

Hooliganism Rowdy, violent or destructive behaviour.

If spectators become over-involved in the expectation of success at a match, this can lead to crowd trouble. This has been a problem for football for the last 50 years. Although acts of **hooliganism** can be serious, they are often sensationalised by the media.

The vast majority of football fans or spectators are not hooligans. This majority expect to attend matches in safety, but this costs money. Crowd trouble at matches needs to be controlled and this causes major concerns for the clubs and footballing authorities.

▲ Crowd trouble at a football match.

The potential for crowd trouble has a negative effect for those watching, especially younger spectators. They could easily be dissuaded from participating in a sport where such activity is commonplace.

✔ Check your understanding

1 What are the main benefits to a sport of increased spectators?
2 What is home-field advantage?
3 What is hooliganism?

Answers are on page 191.

Reasons for hooliganism

Hooliganism can occur in the football grounds, but also in the streets near the ground, in local pubs, on public transport or in city centres. A range of reasons has been suggested for the cause of hooliganism, but none seems to give a full explanation.

One possible cause of hooliganism is rivalry between local teams. Derby matches can inflame the passions of fans, which could spill over into violent behaviour. This is often picked up on by the newspapers and hyped in an attempt to increase sales. However, all sports have derby matches that are played without disturbances between rival fans. In many sports, rival fans often sit together and enjoy the banter.

Crowd trouble has also been linked to alcohol consumption, the argument being that alcohol or drugs lessen inhibitions and make people more open to suggestions. Alcohol is banned at many football stadiums.

Hooliganism is also thought to be a form of tribal behaviour, linked to a gang culture. The group thinks they are protecting their local area or patch from the away fans. This can lead to predetermined, organised violence against another group or gang of fans.

Some forms of spontaneous hooliganism have been blamed on frustration. This could be frustration about their own team's performance, refereeing decisions or the particular circumstances at that club.

Finally, there is some evidence that hooliganism is a type of ritualised behaviour that provides the opportunity for a display of masculinity, and being part of a group. But hooliganism is more than ritualistic, does not solely concern males and does not always involve group membership.

Realistically, there is no single cause of hooligan behaviour in football; It has multiple causes, with each explanation adding something to our understanding of what may cause such behaviour.

Combating hooliganism

During the 1970s and 1980s hooliganism became such a problem for the football authorities that the government, the football governing bodies and the police co-operated to put in place a range of strategies that have resulted in a significant reduction in football-related violence. However, these strategies have come at a cost to the authorities

These strategies are:

- Prevention of known hooligans from travelling to matches by requiring them to report to police stations during match times, or by applying banning orders. But this means that the authorities have to create a list of troublemakers and have knowledge of their existing locations and intentions – all of which costs money.

- Alcohol is not served within most football grounds. Sometimes matches are arranged to kick off early so as to prevent excessive alcohol consumption. The police may require local pubs to close early to prevent alcohol consumption, but this means loss of income for those pubs.

- The introduction of all-seater stadiums for teams playing in the higher divisions reduces the ability of people to move within a stand and allows better control over ticket distribution. But again, there is a cost involved in introducing such facilities.

- Segregation of fans travelling to the match and within the grounds. But there is a policing/stewarding cost and possibly a loss of revenue for the home team where spaces are maintained between rival fans and empty seats on the away side cannot be sold.

- Improved levels of policing and stewarding, allied to better training of stewards, improves crowd control and can lower tension. But the cost to a club of policing home matches in the Premiership can be in the region of £1 million per year.

- Introduction of CCTV cameras at grounds and entrances to stadiums has resulted in more information being gathered about individuals engaged in hooligan behaviour. Known hooligans can be identified and, if appropriate, prevented from entering the ground. But again, there is a cost.

- Poor behaviour by the fans or supporters of a club can result in banning or removing them from competitions, fines, or being forced to play matches away or behind closed doors.

- The football authorities have used high-profile role models to appeal for better supporter behaviour, and have also, through campaigns such

Study hint
Make sure you know three or four reasons for hooliganism.

Study hint
Make sure you know three or four strategies to combat hooliganism.

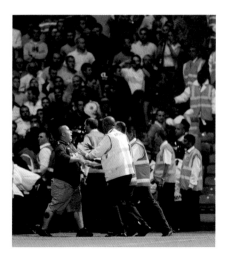

▲ Hooliganism.

as 'Kick racism out of football', attempted to lessen the influence of racist movements among football supporters.

All of the strategies used have cost the authorities and the clubs money. However, the cost is a small price to pay for spectator safety.

▲ Opposing football fans have to be kept separated.

Activity

Read the presentation on hooliganism at:

'Hooliganism' – David Millings

https://prezi.com/jqekeshkz-ir/hooliganism/

✔ Check your understanding

1 Identify three possible negative effects of spectators at matches.
2 Suggest four possible reasons for hooliganism.
3 Give four strategies that have been put in place to reduce hooliganism.

Answers are on page 191.

PRACTICE QUESTIONS

Hooliganism at football matches, both inside and outside stadiums, is a recurring problem.

(a) Describe three steps that have been taken to prevent such acts. (3 marks)
(b) Identify three reasons that have been suggested as to why football should suffer from hooliganism. (3 marks)

Answer can be found on page 192.

Summary

- There is a variety of ethical issues within sport
- Some performers may take prohibited substances; each of which has both positive and negative effects on the performer
- Blood doping is a prohibited method of improving performance
- There are various drugs that are banned by the sporting authorities
- There are advantages and disadvantages to the performer and the sport of taking PEDs
- Spectators have both positive and negative influences at sporting events
- There are various reasons suggested why hooliganism occurs
- There are various strategies that have been put in place to prevent and combat hooliganism

Chapter 6 Health and fitness

Chapter objectives

- Linking participation in physical activity, exercise and sport to fitness, health and well-being
- How exercise can suit the varying needs of different people
- The consequences of a sedentary lifestyle
- Obesity and how it may affect performance in physical activity and sport
- The most suitable body type (somatotypes) for particular sports (or positions within a sport)
- How energy is gained from food and used
- Reasons for having a balanced diet
- The role of carbohydrates, fat, protein, vitamins and minerals
- Reasons for maintaining water balance

Physical, emotional and social health, fitness and well-being

There are several terms and definitions that you need to know in order to fully understand the link between taking part in an activity and what effect it has on health, well-being and fitness.

Although the terms health and fitness are also defined in Chapter 3 on physical training, it is perhaps best to confirm these definitions here:

Health (as per the World Health Organization's definition: 1948) – 'A state of complete physical, mental and social well-being and not merely the absence of disease or infirmity.'

Be aware that 'ill health' refers to being in a state of poor physical, mental and/or social well-being.

Fitness – The ability to meet/cope with the demands of the environment.

By looking at the terms health and fitness, you can see that there is a link between the two. As being 'healthy' includes a 'physical component', you would expect that a healthy person has a well-developed or appropriate level of fitness to allow them to cope with the demands of the environment in which they live and work. This relationship is fully explored in Chapter 3, Physical training.

Key terms

Health A state of complete physical, mental and social well-being and not merely the absence of disease or infirmity.

Fitness The ability to meet/cope with the demands of the environment.

Health and well-being

Health has three distinctive components:

- physical health
- mental health
- social health.

When discussing these three components, it is often useful to group them with the concept of 'well-being'. Thus we often talk about:

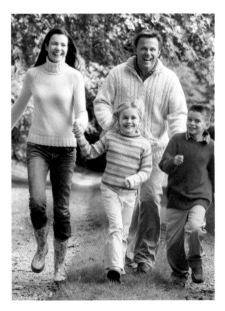

▲ Health and well-being have three components: physical, mental/emotional and social.

Key term

Well-being A mix of physical, social and mental factors that gives people a sense of being comfortable, healthy, and/or happy.

- physical health and well-being
- mental health and well-being
- social health and well-being.

Well-being

Very simply, 'well-being' involves physical, mental and social elements. It is the dynamic mix of the three parts that gives people a sense of being comfortable, healthy and/or happy. Your well-being can refer to how content and/or fulfilled you are in your life, e.g. are you happy with your social life, friends, etc.?

Health and well-being have three components – physical, mental/emotional and social.

Study hint

You need to understand the differences between physical, mental and social well-being. The three together contribute to a person's health. You do not, however, have to distinguish between health and well-being; for example, the effects of exercise on physical health and well-being should be learnt together rather than the health effects and well-being effects separately.

> ### ✔ Check your understanding
>
> Define the terms health, fitness and well-being.
>
> Answers are on page 192.

Physical health and well-being

Physical health and well-being refer to the idea that all of the body's systems are working well, so you are free from illness and injury. You therefore have an ability to carry out everyday tasks. Being active and taking part in exercise can therefore directly benefit your physical health and well-being. In other words, exercise can have a positive impact on the workings within your body.

Taking part in activity/exercise positively affects physical health and well-being as it can:

- improve your heart function (physical health)
- improve the efficiency of the body systems – cardio-vascular system (physical health)
- reduce the risk of some illness, e.g. diabetes (physical health)
- help to prevent the onset of obesity
- enable you to carry out everyday tasks without getting tired (physical well-being)
- provide a feeling that you can comfortably carry out activities and enjoy them (physical well-being).

▲ Carrying out aerobics at a leisure centre or playing recreational sport provide similar benefits to your physical health and well-being as stated previously. Your body adjusts to the exercise and adapts, allowing the body's systems to work more efficiently (physical health). The feeling of being able to complete comfortably and enjoy exercise provides physical well-being.

Mental (emotional) health and well-being

Mental health has been defined by the World Health Organization as: 'a state of well-being in which every individual realises his or her own potential'. An individual with good mental health and well-being can cope with the normal stresses of life, can work productively and fruitfully, and is able to make a contribution to her or his community. Taking an active part in exercise can positively affect your mental health and well-being. Your general state of mind can improve (mental health) and you may 'feel good' about yourself after taking part in a session of suitable exercise (mental well-being).

Taking part in activity/exercise positively affects mental health and well-being as it can:

- reduce stress/tension levels (mental health)
- release feel-good hormones in the body such as serotonin (mental health and well-being)
- enable a person to control their emotions and work productively (mental health).

◀ Many people take part in physical activity to 'remove or release stress from everyday life' thus improving their mental health and well-being. For example, this may be done by visiting the gym after work or meeting friends for a recreational game of badminton at the local leisure centre.

▲ Socialising through sport and exercise is good for social health and well-being.

Social health and well-being

So far we have covered two of the three aspects of health and well-being. The third, social health and well-being, refers to the idea that:

- Basic human needs are being met (food, shelter and clothing).
- The individual has friendship and support, some value in society and is socially active.
- The individual suffers little stress in social circumstances.

Through participating in sport and exercise, individuals get the chance to mix together and socialise. Becoming familiar with people and enjoying friendship allows an individual to feel at ease when being around people and holding conversations. Similarly, organised sport usually takes place in an environment that facilitates basic needs, e.g. wearing a team strip. Social health and well-being is deemed to be a vital component of one's health.

Taking part in physical activity/exercise positively affects social health and well-being as it can:

- provide opportunities to socialise/make friends (social health)
- encourage co-operation skills (social health)
- encourage team-working skills (social health)
- ensure that essential human needs are met (food, shelter, clothing, social well-being).

✔ Check your understanding

Explain how wearing a team strip helps your social health and well-being. Answers are on page 192.

▲ A person who has to carry out manual tasks as part of their job needs to be of an appropriate fitness level to cope with the demands of their work.

Fitness

As mentioned at the start of the chapter, fitness is the 'ability to meet or cope with the demands of the environment'. Thus the fitter you are, the easier you can cope with the demands of your everyday life. These demands may include being productive at work, walking the dog or even running to catch a bus. As you exercise and take part in activities, your body adapts to the demands of the exercise and improves in fitness. This adaptation also lowers the chance of injury occurring. Therefore as your fitness improves you are able to meet the demands of the environment more easily without suffering from fatigue or tiredness.

Improvements in fitness will:

- improve your ability to cope with the demands of your environment
- reduce the chances of you suffering injuries
- make it easier for you to complete physical work, e.g. some people work on their feet all day or carry out manual labour
- make you feel more content/happy (increased well-being).

Activity

Individually or in small groups, match the term to its correct definition.

Term	Definition
Health	Basic human needs are being met (food, shelter and clothing). The individual has friendship and support, some value in society, is socially active and has little stress in social circumstances
Fitness	All body systems working well, free from illness and injury. Ability to carry out everyday tasks
Social health and well-being	A state of complete, physical, mental and social well-being and not merely the absence of disease or infirmity
Mental health and well-being	The ability to meet/cope with the demands of the environment
Physical health and well-being	A 'feel-good' chemical released during exercise
Well-being	A state of well-being in which every individual realises his or her own potential, can cope with the normal stresses of life, can work productively and fruitfully, and is able to make a contribution to his or her community
Serotonin	Involves physical, mental and social well-being. It is the dynamic process of the three parts that gives people a sense of being comfortable, healthy and/or happy.

Answers are on page 195.

PRACTICE QUESTIONS

1. Name and explain two components of well-being. (4 marks)
2. Define health and fitness. (2 marks)
3. Which **one** of the following is an aspect of physical health and well-being?
   A Can cope with the normal stresses of life ☐
   B Individual has friendship and support ☐
   C All body systems working well ☐ (1 mark)

Answers are on page 193.

The consequences of a sedentary lifestyle

'Lifestyle choices' are simply the choices we make about how we live our lives. These could include:

- whether to smoke or not
- whether to drink alcohol or not

Key terms

Physical health and well-being All body systems working well, free from illness and injury. Ability to carry out everyday tasks.

Mental (emotional) health and well-being Defined by the World Health Organization as: 'a state of well-being in which every individual realizes his or her own potential, can cope with the normal stresses of life, can work productively and fruitfully, and is able to make a contribution to her or his community'.

Social health and well-being Basic human needs are being met (food, shelter and clothing). The individual has friendship and support, some value in society, is socially active and has little stress in social circumstances.

Remember that all three of the above components of health and well-being (physical, mental and social) work together.

Study hint

Make sure you are able to link participation in physical activity, exercise and sport to the different types of health/well-being and fitness, e.g. How can taking part in activities improve your social health and well-being?

- whether to exercise or not
- whether to eat a balanced diet or not
- whether to actively seek an education or not.

Individuals of a suitable level of health are able to actively make choices that directly affect the amount of sport and exercise they take part in. Some people choose to do very little exercise. The lifestyle choice about whether to exercise or not significantly affects the health and fitness of an individual.

Sedentary lifestyle

The term 'sedentary' refers to a person's choice to engage in little, or irregular, physical activity. A 'sedentary adult' tends to make an active choice not to take part in exercise or sport. Such a 'choice' can have far-reaching consequences for a person's health and fitness as detailed below.

Key term

Sedentary lifestyle A person's choice to engage in little, or irregular, physical activity.

▲ Leading a sedentary lifestyle is usually a choice, i.e. you could choose to be more active.

Here are some potential consequences of choosing to have a sedentary lifestyle:
- Gaining weight/becoming obese (physical health and well-being).
- Suffering from heart disease (physical health and well-being).
- Suffering from hypertension (physical health and well-being).
- Suffering from diabetes (physical health and well-being).
- Suffering from poor sleep/insomnia (physical health and well-being).
- Suffering from poor self-esteem/confidence (mental health and well-being).
- Feeling tired and lethargic (physical/mental health and well-being).
- Having a lack of friends/poor communication skills (social health and well-being).

The negative effects of a sedentary lifestyle are numerous, yet society still struggles to deal with those people who do not make positive choices in relation to their health and exercise levels. As you have seen previously, a person who follows a sedentary lifestyle may suffer weight gain and become 'obese'.

▲ A person who chooses to follow a sedentary lifestyle may suffer from an inability to sleep (insomnia) and/or lack of self-esteem.

> **✔ Check your understanding**
>
> Name some of the negative effects of choosing to have a sedentary lifestyle.
>
> Answers are on page 192.

Activity

Pair or group debate.

In pairs or small groups discuss the lifestyle choices you make in relation to the amount of activity you do. Answer the following questions:

- Do you exercise regularly (i.e. more than three times a week)?
- What stops or prevents you from making the lifestyle choice to take part in more activity/exercise?
- Do you struggle to sleep or sometimes feel tired for no obvious reason? Could this be because you actually choose not to exercise and therefore often suffer the negative consequences of this?

PRACTICE QUESTIONS

1. What do you understand by the term 'sedentary lifestyle'?　　(1 mark)
2. Describe three possible negative effects of choosing to have a sedentary lifestyle.
　　　　　　(3 marks)

Answers are on page 193.

Obesity and how it may affect performance in physical activity and sport

Obesity is a term used to describe people with a large fat content – usually over 40 per cent body fat. It is caused by an imbalance of calories consumed compared to energy expenditure. Obesity is used to classify people with a Body Mass Index (BMI) of over 30, or 20 per cent or more above ideal weight for height. In simple terms, BMI compares your weight to your height.

▲ In simple terms, you will increase in body weight if your energy intake is greater than your energy expenditure.

Although body mass index is not something you specifically need to know, it is a good measure of whether someone is obese or not. A body mass index chart can show you if you are the correct weight for your height, as shown below.

The general classifications for an individual's BMI are:

● a score of less than 20 = underweight

● a score of 20 – 25 = correct weight

● a score of 25 – 30 = overweight

● a score of 30 + = obese.

Being significantly overweight can affect sporting performance, but it can also affect all three aspects of health and well-being (physical, mental and social).

Obesity and its effects on fitness

It may seem obvious, but carrying a large fat content can affect performance. Although performance in some activities can actually improve due to a large fat content, e.g. sumo wrestling, the effect of being obese is generally negative as it can limit different components of a person's fitness.

Obesity can affect fitness by:

● limiting stamina/cardio-vascular endurance – thus making it difficult to perform any activities of a long duration

● limiting flexibility – making it difficult for performers to use a full range of movement at joints when attempting to perform skills

● limiting agility – making it difficult to change directly quickly

● limiting speed/power – making it hard to react quickly enough or produce force.

Obesity and its effects on health and well-being

In similar ways to how obesity can negatively affect fitness, it also has far-reaching negative effects on a person's health and well-being. Being obese

▲ Body mass index chart.

Key term

Obesity A term used to describe people with a large fat content – caused by an imbalance of calories consumed to energy expenditure. BMI of over 30 or 20 per cent or more above ideal weight for height.

will affect all three components of health and well-being (physical, mental and social).

How obesity can cause ill health (physical):

- It contributes to the development of cancer.
- It contributes to heart disease/heart attacks.
- It contributes to an increase in blood pressure.
- It contributes to the development of diabetes.
- It causes cholesterol levels to rise.
- It can lead to injury.
- It can make the individual feel that they cannot comfortably enjoy activity (well-being).

How obesity can cause ill health (mental/emotional):

- It can lead to depression.
- It can cause a loss of confidence.
- It can make the individual feel like they can't contribute to society (well-being).

How obesity can cause ill health (social):

- It can lead to an inability to socialise.
- It may make the individual feel unable to leave home.
- It may make the individual conscious of how they look and therefore uncomfortable in social situations (well-being).

✔ Check your understanding

In pairs, see if you can remember one negative effect that obesity may have on the three aspects of health and well-being (physical/mental/social). Then see if you can remember two, or even three!

PRACTICE QUESTIONS

1. Define obesity and explain one negative effect that it could have on mental health and well-being. (2 marks)
2. Explain one negative consequence that obesity can have on a person's fitness. (1 mark)

Answers are on page 194.

Rapid recall

As you can see, the physical effects of obesity are numerous. However, you can remember that the physical effects of obesity are **BAD**:
Blood pressure increases
Attacks of the heart can occur
Diabetes may develop

Somatotypes

Somatotype is a method of classifying body types. Three distinctive somatotypes (body shapes) were proposed by William Herbert Sheldon in the 1940s. The particular types of human body shape/physique were classed into the following somatotypes:

- ectomorph
- endomorph
- mesomorph.

These three somatotypes (body shapes) are extremes, i.e. most people do not necessarily display extreme levels of one body type. Many people have characteristics of two, or possibly a mixture of all three, of these shapes.

Ectomorph   Mesomorph   Endomorph

▲ Somatotypes.

Somatotypes for sport

In trying to understand what specific body type is best for an activity, you need to appreciate the characteristics of each somatotype classification and the demands of any given activity. It can be argued that modern-day sport often necessitates a particularly well-developed level of specific fitness with a greater need for strength. Therefore, the link of extreme body shapes to particular sports can be tenuous as most athletes will display a mixture of characteristics. However, the demands of an activity often lend itself to suiting a particular body type.

Ectomorph

An ectomorphic body shape is usually characterised by:

- very thin and lean (usually tall)
- narrow shoulders, hips and chest
- not much fat/muscle
- long arms and legs
- thin face and high forehead.

The thin, lean and tall body shape of an ectomorph is often beneficial for activities where the characteristics of being tall and lean are advantageous. Activities which tend to suit an ectomorphic body shape include:

- high jump
- long jump
- tennis
- endurance activities, e.g. marathon.

Study hint
You should be able to identify the most suitable body type for particular sports (or positions within a sport) and provide reasons for your choice. Remember that body types can be mixed, e.g. swimmers are often ecto/mesomorphic (tall and muscular).

A marathon runner may well benefit from having ectomorphic characteristics as they do not carry much weight (fat and/or muscle). However, for an activity like long jump, which requires power and speed, athletes may well have worked on developing some muscular bulk and therefore display an element of being slightly mesomorphic as well.

Modern sprinters, tennis players and some team sports performers often display the characteristics of an ecto/mesomorph. Usain Bolt is 6 ft 5 inches tall and his long frame characterises elements of an ectomorph. He has however worked on building up muscular bulk to provide him with the power he needs.

Modern-day tennis players are taller and leaner than ever. The characteristics of an ectomorph are beneficial in that serving has become an ever-increasingly important part of the game and serving from height can provide distinctive advantages. It is interesting that at the time of writing all of the world's top four male players are over 6 feet tall.

▲ Andy Murray, Novak Djokovic, Rafael Nadal and Roger Federer are all over 6 ft tall.

Endomorph

An endomorphic body shape is usually characterised by:

- pear-shaped body
- high content of fat
- fat round middle, thighs and upper arms.

The pear-shaped appearance of an endomorph can be beneficial for some activities that simply require bulk. Front row forwards in rugby are often an endomorphic shape, which benefits them when pushing the opposition in the scrum. Similarly, shot putters often display the characteristics of an endomorph, whereby sheer bulk is used in a powerful release of the shot. This is also the case for an activity like sumo wrestling.

▲ A rugby prop using their endomorph characteristics on the field of play.

Mesomorph

A mesomorphic body shape is usually characterised by:

- a wedge shape
- large muscle content
- broad shoulders and thin waist.

The muscular nature of a mesomorph is excellent for producing power and strength. They are not necessarily over-burdened with muscle (i.e. can hardly move due to having so much muscle) but tend to have distinctive muscle definition in the chest and shoulders creating a wedge-like body shape. Such a shape is beneficial in sprinting whereby the force generated at the shoulders can allow the arms to 'pump' (allowing the legs to move faster). Equally, a weightlifter will have high upper body muscle bulk to provide the force to lift and hold a very heavy weight. Many rugby players (league and union) display mesomorphic characteristics allowing them to generate force when making contact with their opponents.

> ### Activity
>
> In small groups learn to appreciate the importance of the muscular upper body of a sprinter (mesomorph). Jog slowly on the spot. Start to pump your arms with power whilst trying to keep your legs jogging slowly. You should realise that the faster and more powerful the arms work, the faster and more powerful the legs work.

Key terms

Somatotype A classification of body type – ectomorph, endomorph or mesomorph.

Endomorph A somatotype characterised by a pear-shaped body/fatness with wide hips and narrow shoulders.

Ectomorph A somatotype characterised by being tall and thin with narrow shoulders and narrow hips.

Mesomorph A somatotype characterised by muscular appearance with wide shoulders and narrow hips.

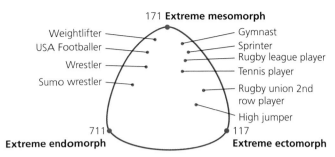

▲ This diagram provides a representation of what somatotype tends to suit certain sports.

✅ Check your understanding

Describe the three somatotypes.
Answers are on page 193.

Activity

1 What body type would you say you were? Therefore, what sporting activities does your body shape stereotypically suit? Do you actually play/perform in these activities? Compare with classmates.

2 For the following sporting activities, suggest the stereotypical body shape that would suit that activity:

Activity	Body type required
Hammer thrower	
Pole vaulter	
400 m sprinter	
Marathon runner	

Answer to question 2 is on page 195.

PRACTICE QUESTIONS

1. With references to a sporting activity of your choice, explain why an ectomorph body type may be beneficial.   (3 marks)
2. Sprinters often have wide muscular shoulders and a low fat content. What body type is this?
- Mesomorph ☐
- Ectomorph ☐
- Endomorph ☐ (1 mark)

Answers are on page 194.

Energy use, diet, nutrition and hydration

Kilocalories or calories (energy from food) are important for providing energy to carry out everyday activities and allow the body to function normally. Our bodies require energy for everything we do – for growth, repair, development and for movement when performing activities like running, swimming and walking.

Energy is measured in calories or kilocalories (kcal). These calories are obtained from the food and drink we consume. Therefore, the more calories we consume through our food the more energy we have to use. If we do not use the calories they get stored in the body, causing weight gain.

Average calorie requirements

The average adult male requires 2500 kcal/day and the average adult female requires 2000 kcal/day. However, these figures are dependent upon several factors:

Study hint
Make sure you know how many calories the average adult male and female need per day.

▲ Olympic swimming legend Michael Phelps was rumoured to consume as much as 12,000 calories a day during his gruelling training schedule in preparation for the Olympics.

▲ McDonald's states that a Big Mac contains 508 calories.

- The age of the individual (after age 25, the calorie needs of individuals start to fall).
- The gender (as you can see, men usually need more calories).
- The height of the individual (taller people tend to require more calories).
- The energy expenditure (in other words, how much exercise the individual does – the more exercise, the more calories are required).
- The basal metabolic rate (BMR). This is basically how fast energy is being used. It can vary from individual to individual.

It may seem obvious, but the calorie intake required to provide energy for a day will vary depending on what you are doing that day. Some top-class athletes need to eat much more than the average suggested intake in order to cope with the demands of their training schedule.

✔ Check your understanding

What is the suggested calorie intake per day for an average adult male and female?

Answers are on page 193.

It is interesting to note that an individual sleeping uses approximately 1 calorie per minute, 3–4 when walking and 8–10 when jogging fast.

Nutrition – reasons for having a balanced diet

The food and drink you consume contain calories but are also made up of varying constituents. A balanced diet is eating the right amount of calories to deal with the energy that will be needed (suitable intake to match energy expenditure/exercise). However, it is also eating different food types to provide suitable nutrients, vitamins and minerals. Minerals are inorganic substances which assist the body with many of its functions, e.g. bone formation (calcium). Vitamins are organic substances that are required for many essential processes in the body, e.g. Vitamin A for structure and function of the skin.

▲ An English breakfast, Cornish pasty for lunch and fish and chips for an evening meal. These are popular British meals but would they constitute a 'balanced diet' providing the body with the nutrients, vitamins and minerals it needs?

Aiming for a 'balanced diet'

Unfortunately, there is no one food that contains all the nutrients the body needs. Some foods have particular properties which benefit the body:

- High fibre cereals and whole grains provide fibre, which prevents constipation and can help reduce blood cholesterol (fatty deposits).

- Milk, cheese and other dairy products provide calcium (a mineral), which is good for nerve and muscle function as well as teeth and bone growth.

- Iron (mineral) rich foodstuffs like liver help the immune system and assist in the production of red blood cells which carry oxygen.

- Vitamin A (for skin function and growth) is found in dairy products like cheese.

- Oily fish, eggs and butter provide Vitamin D to help bones.

- Vitamin C is found in citrus fruit, broccoli and liver and aids the immune system, skin elasticity and blood vessel function.

- Various types of Vitamin B are found in whole grains, nuts, eggs and fish to assist with the functions of the body.

A truly 'balanced' diet contains lots of different types of food and would normally involve an individual consuming a mixture of carbohydrate, protein and fat from a variety of sources. The ideal 'mix' of different foods should also include green vegetables and fruit to provide the suitable nutrients, vitamins and minerals required. As a rough guide, you should aim for five portions of fruit and vegetables per day. When measuring vegetables, a 'fist size' portion is often regarded as one portion. The ideal mix of foods is sometimes referred to as the 'seven classes of food': carbohydrate, fat, protein, fibre, **vitamins**, **minerals** and water.

> **Activity**
>
> Discuss last night's evening meal with a partner. Did either of you consume all seven of the classes of food? Did you manage to consume five portions of fruit and vegetables yesterday? In France, the government recommends ten portions of fruit and vegetables a day!

▲ A mix of fruit and vegetables provide the body with vitamins and minerals.

Answers are on page 193.

Key terms

Balanced diet Eating the right amount (for energy expended)/ the right amount of calories/ eating according to how much you exercise/eating different food types to provide suitable nutrients, vitamins and minerals.

Minerals Inorganic substances that assist the body with many of its functions.

Vitamins Organic substances that are required for many essential processes in the body.

Study hint

Make sure you know the percentage recommendations for carbohydrate, fat and protein.

▲ Pasta is a food source rich in complex carbohydrate – providing energy.

Key terms

Carbohydrate Food source that acts as the body's preferred energy source.

Fat Food source that provides energy at low intensities.

So why should you strive to have a balanced diet?

- Unused energy is stored as **fat**, which could cause obesity (particularly saturated fat found in deep-fried food).
- Suitable amounts of energy should be consumed to be made available for the exercise and activity carried out.
- The human body needs nutrients for energy, growth and hydration (see hydration below).

> ✔ **Check your understanding**
>
> What are the seven classes of food? What is a truly 'balanced' diet?
> Answers are on page 193.

PRACTICE QUESTIONS

1. An adult man averages a daily intake of 3500 kcal per day. Is this too much or too little based on recommended guidelines? Justify your answer. (2 marks)
2. If an adult female is in training for an event, why might she eat and drink more calories than the recommended daily intake? (2 marks)

Answers are on page 194.

Carbohydrates, fat, protein, vitamins and minerals

As you have discovered already, a balanced diet contains seven elements: carbohydrate, fat, protein, fibre, vitamins, minerals and water. With specific reference to carbohydrates, fat and protein, the recommended percentages that your diet should contain is:

- 55–60 per cent carbohydrate
- 25–30 per cent fat, and
- 15–20 per cent protein.

Carbohydrates

Carbohydrates are the main and preferred energy source for all types of exercise, of all intensities. The body requires a supply of glucose as an energy fuel and carbohydrate acts as the main source of glucose. Thus for an athlete requiring energy, carbohydrate is a very important part of their diet. There are many types of carbohydrate (simple and complex) that can be consumed. Bread, pasta and potatoes provide valuable sources of starch, which is a complex carbohydrate.

Fat

Fat is also an energy source and helps to carry vitamins in the body, e.g. Vitamin A. It provides more energy than carbohydrates – in fact more than double the amount that carbohydrate provides. The key, however, is that fat can only be used as an energy source at low intensity, e.g. walking, light jogging and so on. Although fat is a concentrated energy source it does come in two forms – 'saturated fat' (usually animal fat) and 'unsaturated fat' (usually vegetable fat/oils).

Although many people perceive fat as a bad or unhealthy part of a diet, you do in fact need to consume 25–30 per cent fat within your normal diet. However, a high fat intake (particularly saturated fat) is strongly linked to many health risks. These include:

- high cholesterol
- heart disease
- narrowing of arteries due to fat deposits.

Study hint

Don't forget that fat can provide more energy than carbohydrate BUT only when you are working at a low intensity.

▲ Saturated fat tends to be derived from animal sources and can cause health risks.

Protein

Protein is predominantly for growth and repair of body tissues. It also has a small part to play in providing energy. The main sources of protein within the diet are meat, eggs, fish, dairy products, nuts and cereals. For some athletes, particularly those that lift weights and do strength/power activities, a diet rich in protein is beneficial to help them with the development and repair of muscle tissue.

▲ Food sources that are rich in protein.

Key term

Protein Food source which is predominantly for growth and repair of body tissues.

Activity

Take note of your daily intake of food. Using the wrappers and packaging try to keep track of the amount of carbohydrate, fat and protein you consume. Does your intake conform to the recommended levels? You could also try to design a suitable daily intake containing the recommended percentages of carbohydrate, fat and protein.

Vitamins and minerals

Vitamin and mineral intake comes from foodstuffs such as fruit and vegetables. Vitamins and minerals are needed for maintaining the efficient working of the body systems and general health.

Vitamins are 'organic substances' that are required for many essential processes in the body, e.g. Vitamin A for structure and function of the skin. Minerals are 'inorganic substances' which assist the body with many of its functions, e.g. bone formation (calcium).

Water

Water consumption is often neglected by many people but it is a vital component of a healthy diet. As water makes up more than half of the human body, it is necessary to maintain **hydration** levels (water balance) as it assists in how the body functions generally. It helps with reactions, lubrication and also plays a big part in maintaining correct body temperature. It is also important to note that the amount of water you should drink a day depends on several factors:

- The environment you are in, e.g. you would need more water in a desert.
- The temperature in which you are in – the hotter it is, the more you sweat and therefore you need more water.
- The amount of exercise/activity you are doing – exercising means that you need to replace water (**rehydration**).

It is vital that water consumption prevents '**dehydration**'. This is when there is an excessive loss of body water interrupting the functioning of the body.

It is important to remain hydrated as it prevents the effects of dehydration.

Dehydration in the body has many harmful effects:

- The blood thickens (increased viscosity), which slows blood flow down.
- The heart rate increases which means that the heart has to work harder. This can cause an irregular heart rate (rhythm).
- The body temperature is likely to increase, meaning that the body may overheat.
- Reaction time increases. In other words, it gets slower and general reactions are poorer. This of course means that decisions made may be negatively affected.
- An individual may suffer muscle fatigue and/or muscle cramps.

Key terms

Dehydration Excessive loss of body water interrupting the function of the body.

Hydration Having enough water (water balance) to enable normal functioning of the body.

Rehydration Consuming water to restore hydration.

▲ The recommended daily intake of water is approximately eight large glasses a day to maintain hydration levels.

Activity

1 In the table below, match the correct term with the correct definition.

Term	Definition
Dehydration	Consuming water to restore hydration.
Hydration	Excessive loss of body water interrupting the function of the body.
Rehydration	Having enough water (water balance) to enable normal functioning of the body.

2 Take note of the amount of water you consume in a 24-hour period. Does it conform to the recommended daily intake of eight large glasses? Compare your results with classmates.

Answer to question 1 is on page 195.

✔ Check your understanding

1 What are the recommended percentages for carbohydrate, fat and protein within your diet?
2 What is the role of vitamins and minerals within the diet?
3 What do the terms hydration, dehydration and rehydration mean?

Answers are on page 193.

Summary

- Exercise can be used to suit the varying needs of different people
- Exercise can affect physical, mental and social health and well-being
- A sedentary lifestyle is a choice and has many negative effects
- Obesity is a consequence of a sedentary lifestyle and can affect all aspects of health and performance
- There are stereotypical and suitable body types (somatotypes) for particular sports (or positions within a sport)
- Energy is gained from food. If more energy is taken than used there will be weight gain (and vice versa)
- A balanced diet contains the seven classes of food: carbohydrate, fat, protein, fibre, vitamins, minerals and water
- The following have specific roles: carbohydrates (energy), fat (energy), protein (growth and repair), vitamins and minerals (efficient functions)
- Water balance prevents dehydration and the resultant consequences, e.g. thicker blood

PRACTICE QUESTIONS

1. An adult consumes 40 per cent fat in a day. Does this conform to the recommended daily intake? Justify your answer. (2 marks)
2. Explain three different negative consequences of becoming dehydrated. (3 marks)
3. Explain the main roles of carbohydrate, fat and protein. (3 marks)

Answers are on page 194.

Chapter 7 Use of data

As part of your GCSE in Physical Education, you will be required in both of your examinations to show knowledge and understanding of data analysis. In simple terms, the skills you will need to show can be summarised as:

- Show an understanding of the types of data.
- Show an understanding of how data is collected.
- Demonstrate an ability to present data in various formats.
- Demonstrate an understanding of how to analyse data, e.g. break it down into smaller parts.
- Demonstrate an understanding of how to evaluate data, e.g. does the data show anything, any trends, any interesting points.

It is important to note that there is no one topic area that will definitely be examined using data. All topic areas within the specification could be referred to with 'data based' questions. This chapter provides you with some further information to help to prepare you for your examinations.

Show an understanding of the types of data

Your ability to show an understanding of the types of data is with particular reference to the terms:

- quantitative data
- qualitative data.

Quantitative data deals with numbers. You can remember the meaning of this by using the expression: 'Quantitative data deals with quantities'.

By definition, quantitative data is a measurement that can be quantified as a number, e.g. time in seconds, or goals scored. There is no opinion expressed (qualitative); it is a fact/objective.

Most topic areas within the specification could potentially be examined through questions which refers to numbers/quantities/amounts. For example:

- Fitness tests produce numerical scores.
- Heart rate is measured in beats per minute and can therefore be plotted on a graph.
- Engagement patterns of different social groups could actually be shown as numerical amounts or percentages.

Qualitative data on the other hand deals with opinions. It is subjective as it allows for different people to express different viewpoints.

By definition, qualitative data is more of a subjective than an objective appraisal. It involves opinions relating to the quality of a performance rather than the quantity. Whereas a fitness test could produce a numerical score (quantitative), the person carrying it out may well suggest that they 'did poorly'. This expression of opinion is qualitative.

Key terms

Quantitative data Data that can be quantified as a number, e.g. time in seconds, or goals scored. There is no opinion expressed (qualitative); it is a fact.

Qualitative data Data which is subjective, involving opinions relating to the quality of a performance rather than the quantity.

Most topics within the specification could include qualitative data within the examinations. For example:

- the opinions expressed about the positive or negative impact of commercialisation on a spectator
- the opinions expressed about the merits of extrinsic motivation
- the opinions expressed by different people about what a diet should contain.

Show an understanding of how data is collected

It is also important that as a student of GCSE Physical Education you can identify how quantitative and qualitative data is collected.

Quantitative data involving quantities and amounts tends to be gathered using the following methods:

- Questionnaires – a series of questions, whereby the number of people who give a certain answer can be expressed as a quantity.
- Surveys – for example, in the television programme *Family Fortunes*, the host uses the number of people who expressed a particular answer.

However, with specific reference to physical education, it is also likely that other data collection could be used. For example:

- heart rate monitors to measure heart rate
- stopwatches to gain a time, e.g. in the Illinois agility test
- metre ruler to gain a score, e.g. in the reaction time test.

Qualitative data involving opinions is generally gathered through the following methods:

- interviews
- observations.

With specific reference to physical education, you may well see from an observation that a performer appears to be over aroused, or you may interview a participant who expresses their delight at their score after a fitness test.

Demonstrate an ability to present data in various formats

As previously mentioned, you may be required to present data as part of your examinations. In simple terms, this could involve looking at information provided to you and turning it into a different format. The specification states that those 'formats' could include:

- plotting a basic line chart
- plotting a basic bar chart
- labelling the x and y axis correctly on a chart.

At this point it is perhaps best to provide some detail about line charts, bar charts and labelling axes.

Check your understanding

Explain what qualitative and quantitative data are and identify some methods to collect the data. Answers are on page 196.

Activity

In pairs, discuss the last time you carried out fitness tests. What did you score in the test (quantitative) and how was the data collected? How did you feel you did in those tests (qualitative)? Interview each other to collect the qualitative data.

PRACTICE QUESTION

What do you understand by the terms qualitative and quantitative data?

(2 marks)

Answer is on page 196.

Key terms

Line chart The use of plotted points (markers) to show data, which are joined together by a line.

Bar chart The use of rectangular bars which show the data quantities.

A **line chart** involves plotting points (markers) onto graph paper so that the points (markers) can be joined together. An example is shown below; however, note that the source of where the data has come from has been made up.

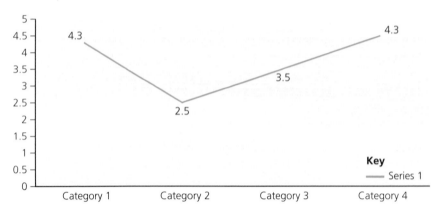

▲ A line chart.

A **bar chart** is similar to a line chart; however, the amount up to the plotted point is shaded in to show a 'bar area'. The rectangular shaded areas show the amount. An example is shown below, using the same plotting points as used in the line chart.

▲ A bar chart.

In terms of labelling axes, it is important to remember a couple of terms:

- The X axis goes across – so remember X (a cross).
- The Y axis goes up the side – the letter Y points up.
- In complex terms, the 'independent' variable goes on the **x axis** (the bottom horizontal one) and the 'dependent' variable goes on the **y axis** (the left side, vertical one). In more simple terms, time is often the independent variable. So, for example, if a graph shows heart rate over a period of time, heart rate is the thing you really want to know, so it is the dependent variable. Other examples include: steps walked per day. You want to know the steps walked so this is the dependent variable (y axis). The days are the independent variable (x axis).

Key terms

X axis Shows the independent variable.

Y axis Shows the dependent variable (the thing you are measuring, e.g. heart rate).

Within this chapter we are going to use an example from the topic area of motivation. Given the information below, it is suggested that you practise carrying out the tasks on graph paper.

PRACTICE QUESTION

The question read: During today's training what do you think is motivating you more to train harder – intrinsic reward (e.g. personal pride) or extrinsic reward (e.g. winning a medal). The following quantitative responses were gained as scores out of 10.

N.B. As the level of motivation is the thing being studied, this is the dependent variable – y axis.

Week	Answers given
1	Intrinsic 3 Extrinsic 7
2	Intrinsic 4 Extrinsic 6
3	Intrinsic 5 Extrinsic 5
4	Intrinsic 5 Extrinsic 5
5	Intrinsic 8 Extrinsic 2

a) Plot the data onto the graph paper below showing athlete responses over the five-week period. You should use a line graph method and should label the axes appropriately.

b) Plot the same data onto the graph paper below showing athlete responses over the five-week period. You should use a bar chart method and should label the axes appropriately.

N.B. The answers are on page 197. Compare your responses to those at the back and try again if necessary. Have plenty of goes using different data sources.

Demonstrate an understanding of how to analyse and evaluate data

In your exam, you may be asked to analyse and/or evaluate data. Analyse means to break things down into smaller parts or identify the relevant parts. Evaluate involves deciding upon the worth of or reasons for something.

To make this simpler look at the following example:

An athlete's heart rate was recorded before and during exercise at one-minute intervals.

2 minutes before	68 beats per minute (bpm)
1 minute before	74 bpm
At the start	78 bpm
1 minute into exercise	84 bpm
2 minutes into exercise	88 bpm
3 minutes into exercise	105 bpm
4 minutes into exercise	106 bpm
5 minutes into exercise	106 bpm
6 minutes into exercise	107 bpm

Analyse the data shown to plot a line graph showing the heart rates 1 minute before exercise, at the start of exercise, and 1, 2, 3, 4, 5 and 6 minutes into exercise.

In this specific example you would be required to analyse the data shown and prepare a graph showing the desired points. This would look like the following:

An evaluation of this graph could well ask you to evaluate what the data shows. For example, 'Looking at the heart rate during exercise, describe what intensity the athlete has been working at'.

In this case, the data demonstrates a slight rise in intensity at the start of exercise, which appears to be levelling off at 3 minutes.

Remember that analysis involves breaking data down into smaller parts or picking out the relevant data. Evaluation involves looking at something's worth or what it actually shows.

The following graph shows the percentage of females/males (of differing ages) that participate regularly in sporting activity.

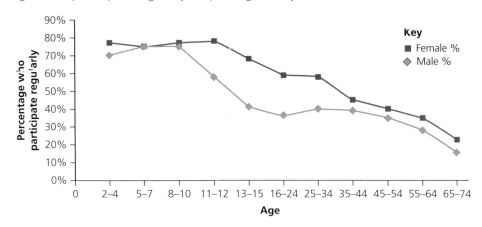

With this kind of graph, you could be asked a range of questions. For example, you may encounter ones which involve evaluation:

1   At what age do participation rates of girls match those of boys?
2   At what age are participation rates for boys the highest?
3   At what age are participation rates for females the lowest?

Answers:

1   5–7 years
2   11–12 years
3   65–74 years

Chapter 8 Non-examined assessment

As part of your GCSE in Physical Education you are required to complete a non-examined assessment (or NEA for short). You may well refer to this as your 'practical'.

Your NEA contributes 40 per cent of your overall mark, with your examinations making up the remaining 60 per cent. You will have to choose to be assessed in three different activities from the official activity list below and complete an analysis and improvement task on one of your chosen activities.

In choosing from the list below, be aware that you must choose:

- an individual activity
- a team activity, and
- another of your choice, e.g. badminton (individual), football (team), tennis (other).

The official activity list

Team activities

- Association football (cannot be five-a-side or futsal)
- Badminton doubles (cannot be assessed with singles badminton)
- Basketball
- Camogie (cannot be assessed with hurling)
- Cricket
- Dance (can only be used for one activity)
- Gaelic football
- Handball
- Hockey (must be field hockey. Cannot be assessed as ice hockey or roller hockey)
- Hurling (cannot be assessed with camogie)
- Lacrosse
- Netball
- Rowing (cannot be assessed with sculling, canoeing or kayaking. This can only be used for one activity)
- Rugby league (cannot be assessed with rugby union or rugby sevens. Cannot be tag rugby)
- Rugby union (can be assessed as sevens or fifteen-a-side. Cannot be assessed with rugby league and cannot be tag rugby)
- Squash doubles (cannot be assessed with singles squash)
- Table tennis doubles (cannot be assessed with singles table tennis)
- Tennis doubles (cannot be assessed with singles tennis)
- Volleyball

Individual activity list

- Amateur boxing
- Athletics (two different events/groups, e.g. sprint and jump)
- Badminton singles (cannot be assessed with doubles badminton)
- Canoeing/kayaking (slalom) (cannot be assessed in both canoeing and kayaking. Cannot be assessed with canoeing/kayaking sprint, rowing or sculling)
- Canoeing/kayaking (sprint) (cannot be assessed in both canoeing and kayaking. Cannot be assessed with canoeing/kayaking slalom, rowing or sculling)
- Cycling track or road cycling only (cannot be assessed in track cycling and in road cycling)
- Dance solo (can only be used for one activity)
- Diving (platform diving only)
- Golf
- Gymnastics (artistic) (floor routines and apparatus only. Cannot be rhythmic gymnastics)
- Equestrian
- Rock climbing (can be indoor or outdoor climbing)
- Sculling (cannot be assessed with rowing, canoeing or kayaking)
- Skiing (outdoor/indoor on snow. Cannot be assessed with snowboarding. Must not be on dry slopes)
- Snowboarding (outdoor/indoor on snow. Cannot be assessed with skiing. Must not be on dry slopes)
- Squash (cannot be assessed with doubles squash)
- Swimming (cannot be synchronised swimming. Cannot be personal survival. Cannot be lifesaving)
- Table tennis singles (cannot be assessed with doubles table tennis)
- Tennis singles (cannot be assessed with doubles tennis)
- Trampolining

Disability/specialist activities

N.B. Students without a disability cannot be assessed in these activities.

- Blind cricket
- Goal ball
- Powerchair football (cannot be assessed with wheelchair football)
- Table cricket
- Wheelchair basketball
- Wheelchair football (cannot be assessed with powerchair football)
- Wheelchair rugby

Specialist individual activity list

- Boccia
- Polybat

Choosing your activities

In choosing your three activities, remember that you can only perform (play) in these activities. You are not able to coach or officiate. Therefore, you must choose wisely with the intention to maximise the marks that you will eventually be given. Please also note that there are a few activity combinations that are not possible. These are included in the list above – e.g. you cannot do rugby union and rugby league or singles and doubles badminton.

All activities are scored out of 25, with:

- 10 marks being awarded for Part 1: your performance in progressive drills/practices and
- 15 marks being awarded for Part 2: your ability to perform in a fully competitive context.

Please see AQA's specification for full details of how marks are awarded.

▲ Three activities must be chosen and must come from an individual activity, a team activity and another of your choice.

There are a few key points to consider:

The skills being performed in **Part 1** should allow you to show yourself in the best possible light, e.g. a very simple passing drill in football will not score very high marks. You may start with a simple drill but it must progress to challenge you and show your ability to, for example, receive the ball on the move and pass accurately to other players on the move over varying distances.

When performing **Part 2**, the level of the competition will be taken into account when assessing you. Therefore, if you are playing against very easy opposition it may not help you score a high mark.

Assessment

Assessment of your three chosen activities will be carried out by your teachers but will also be moderated by external AQA staff.

It can be difficult capturing footage of yourself performing at your best. If you are asked by your teacher to do so, please remember a few simple rules:

- You should be seen performing at the highest level possible – ask your coach to make the practices harder and harder to show you being tested.
- Don't forget it must be the full recognised version of the activity for Part 2 – e.g. 5-a-side football will not do!
- It must be clear and the person watching it must be able to actually see you!
- You may need to gain several examples from several different drills in training and several different competitive contexts.
- Team sports require a 'player cam' approach for Part 2, i.e. the camera should follow you but also be on a wide enough setting to see what is going on in the game.
- The mark awarded will not be based purely on the level you are performing at – e.g. even if you are an international performer, there must be an appropriate amount of evidence of you actually performing.
- It is sometimes advisable to include 'voice over' on top of the footage. For example, in a game of rugby there may be 30 bodies covered in mud! In this case it will help if you commentate as to where you are and what you are doing.

Part 1

The main factors that you will be assessed on in Part 1 are:

- The quality of technique shown and whether it is maintained for all skills and throughout all practices.
- Your ability to make decisions in both predetermined (expected) and spontaneous (unexpected) situations.
- The number of errors in your skill production.
- How adaptive you are (in other words how you change what you are doing) when faced with progressively challenging situations, e.g. as the practice progresses.
- Your fitness level (in sports like cycling and rowing).

▲ Skill drills being performed for Part 1.

Part 2

The main areas that you will be assessed on in Part 2 are:

▲ Full competitive context for Part 2.

- Your ability to make successful and effective tactical and strategic decisions.
- Your level of contribution – is it sustained for the whole activity?
- Your level of technical consistency in the performance of all skills.
- Selecting the appropriate skills to use at the right time.
- Your ability to play a position (in team sports).
- Your ability to outwit opponents (where appropriate).
- Your choreography skills (in dance).

Analysis and evaluation task

The analysis and evaluation task is completed as a piece of coursework that you can work on at school/college and/or at home. It can be completed at any point during the two years of your studies at GCSE. It is submitted towards the end of the second year (usually Year 11).

The analysis and evaluation task that you have to complete is marked out of 25.

This is split into two separate sections:

- Analysis
- Evaluation

▲ Students undertaking written assessment.

For this element of coursework, you are required to analyse and evaluate a performance in one activity from the specification. This can be an analysis/evaluation of one of your own performances or it could be on the performance of another person. It must, however, be in relation to an activity that is from the specification.

N.B. You can choose to present your work in a written format or a verbal format. If you use a verbal format, you will need to be videoed carrying it out.

▲ Submit written work or carry out a verbal interview.

Analysis – 15 marks

Whether you analyse your own or another person's performance, you are required to analyse the performance to suggest two strengths and two weaknesses, referring to recent competitive performance(s) in the chosen activity.

- **Strength 1** should be a fitness component (e.g. speed, or something relevant to the chosen activity). You will need to justify how it has helped in the performance(s). The fitness components in the specification are:
  - agility
  - balance
  - cardio-vascular endurance (aerobic power)
  - co-ordination
  - flexibility
  - muscular endurance
  - power/explosive strength (anaerobic power)
  - reaction time
  - strength (maximal, static, dynamic and explosive)
  - speed.
- **Strength 2** should be a specific skill/technique (from those listed in the activity criteria) or tactic/strategy/aspect of choreography (as appropriate). If you choose a skill, e.g. shooting in football, you should refer to the technique used and how that technique benefited performance, e.g. kept head over the ball to keep the shot low. If you choose to use a tactic/strategy you must explain how it benefited performance. If an aspect of choreography is chosen, reference can be made to how the choreographed movement benefited performance of the dance.
- In choosing these strengths, it is very important that you fully justify your two choices, e.g. what impact did they have on performance? Where possible, try to use activity specific terminology/terms within your answer.
- **Weakness 1** should be a fitness component (e.g. power, or something relevant to the chosen activity – from the list above). You will need to justify how it has negatively affected performance.

- **Weakness 2** should be a specific skill/technique (from those listed in the activity criteria) or tactic/strategy/aspect of choreography (as appropriate).

Evaluation – 10 marks

You are now required to devise an action plan that evaluates how the weaknesses can be improved. All of the evaluation will make use of theoretical topics from the specification.

Remember that improvement does not actually have to happen. You are suggesting what would happen if you were to do these things!

▲ Could weight training or continuous training be appropriate training types to improve upon the identified weaknesses?

Answers

Chapter 1a Applied anatomy and physiology

Check your understanding

Page 3

1 We need support to give our body shape, keep us upright and to keep the muscles and organs in place.

2 The skeleton produces red blood cells that transport carbon dioxide and oxygen to and from the lungs. White blood cells are produced and help fight off infections.

3 Muscles attach to the bones of the skeleton and pull the bones, which causes movement.

Page 3

1 Joint capsule provides stability; ligaments join bones to bone.

2 Synovial fluid is produced from the synovial membrane and works as a lubricant; bursae are bags of fluid that help reduce friction.

3 Tendons attach muscles to bone.

Page 8

1 Humerus, radius and ulna.

2 Ball and socket joint, e.g. hip or shoulder.

3 Dorsiflexion and plantar flexion.

Page 9

1 Tibia and femur.

2 Knee, elbow and ankle.

3 Flexion, extension, adduction, abduction, rotation.

Practice questions

Page 4

1 Join bone to bone.

2 Cover ends of bone to protect.

3 Release/produce synovial fluid – lubricates the joint.

Page 9

1 Plantar flexion – toes pointed/move down; dorsiflexion – toes pulled up.

2 Extension.

3 Abduction – arm/limb away from mid-line; adduction – arm/limb towards mid-line.

Activity

Page 4

Cartilage – on ends of bones – protective covering.

Capsule – tough fibrous tissue – supports/strengthens joint.

Synovial membrane – releases synovial fluid – lubricates joint.

Synovial fluid – lubricant – reduces friction.

Bursae – fluid filled bags – reduce friction.

Page 7

Flexion – move forwards.

Extension – move backwards.

Abduction – move away from the body.

Adduction – move back towards the body.

Rotation – turn hand/arm in and/or out.

Page 9

Shoulder – flexion – arm forwards, extension, arm back, abduction – arm out to side, adduction – arm back to body from side, rotation – hand/arm turn in/out.

Elbow – flexion – arm bends at elbow, extension – arm straightens at elbow.

Hip – flexion – whole leg moves forward when in standing position, extension – whole leg returns from flexed to standing position.

Knee – flexion – leg bends at knee, extension – leg straightens at knee.

Ankle – plantar flexion – toes pointed away from leg, dorsiflexion – toes pointing up towards leg.

Chapter 1b The structure and function of the cardio-respiratory system

Check your understanding

Page 11

1 Trap dirt and dust.

2 Bronchi conduct air from trachea to lungs; bronchioles conduct air from bronchi to alveoli.

3 Keep trachea open.

4 Provide surface for diffusion of gases/gas exchange.

Page 12

1 Because concentration of oxygen is higher in alveoli than in blood capillaries.

2 Thin cells walls/membranes; short distance between membranes; large surface area; layer of moisture; rich blood supply/lots of capillaries.

3 Transport oxygen (as oxyhaemoglobin; also transports carbon dioxide).

Page 13

1 Diaphragm and intercostal muscles.

2 Pectorals.

3 The diaphragm and intercostals relax and the chest cavity returns to its normal/resting size.

4 Abdominals.

Page 14

1 Volume of air breathed in or out at rest.

2 Inspiratory reserve volume.

3 Residual volume.

Page 15

1 Recoil/return to shape.

2 Veins.

3 Increasing diameter of artery.

4 Allow diffusion.

Page 17

1 Systole – contraction; diastole – relaxation.

2 Prevent backflow of blood.

3 From right atrium; through atrioventricular valve; to right ventricle; systole; through pulmonary artery to lungs.

4 From lungs through pulmonary veins; into left atrium; through atrioventricular valves; to left ventricle.

Page 17

1 Volume of blood leaving the heart in one minute.

2 Cardiac output = stroke volume × heart rate.

3 Volume of blood leaving the heart per beat.

4 4900 mls/min or 4.9 L/min.

Practice questions

Page 11

Trachea; Bronchi; Bronchioles.

Page 12

Gases move from area of high concentration to lower concentration;

Oxygen out of alveoli; carbon dioxide into alveoli.

Page 13

1 Diaphragm and intercostal muscles contract; chest volume increases; air moves from higher pressure into the lungs.

2 Inspiration assisted by pectorals; expiration assisted by abdominals.

Page 14

TV increases; IRV decreases; ERV decreases.

Page 17

Deoxygenated blood; from RV into pulmonary artery; to lungs; gas exchange/becomes oxygenated; pulmonary veins; left atria.

Page 18

Cardiac output – volume of blood leaving the heart per minute.

Stroke volume – volume of blood leaving the heart per beat.

Cardiac output = stroke volume x heart rate.

Activity

page 10

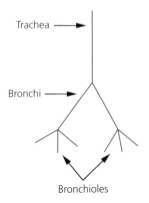

Trachea →

Bronchi →

Bronchioles

Page 11

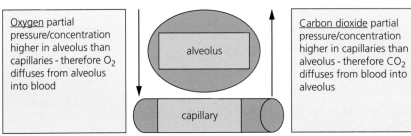

Oxygen partial pressure/concentration higher in alveolus than capillaries - therefore O_2 diffuses from alveolus into blood

alveolus

capillary

Carbon dioxide partial pressure/concentration higher in capillaries than alveolus - therefore CO_2 diffuses from blood into alveolus

Page 12

Any four of:

1 Large surface area – large
2 Thin membranes – thin
3 Short diffusion pathway – short
4 Layer of moisture – moist
5 Rich blood supply – blood

Page 14

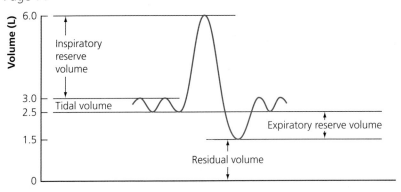

Volume (L)

6.0

Inspiratory reserve volume

3.0
2.5
Tidal volume

1.5
Residual volume

Expiratory reserve volume

0

Page 16

Right atrium	Left atrium
Right ventricle	Left ventricle

Page 16

Chapter 1c Anaerobic and aerobic exercise

Check your understanding

Page 20

1 Aerobic – with oxygen; anaerobic – without oxygen.

2 Glucose + Oxygen $\rightarrow$ Energy + Carbon Dioxide + Water.

3 Waste product of anaerobic exercise/causes fatigue.

4 Glucose $\rightarrow$ Energy + Lactic acid.

Page 21

1 Excess Post-exercise Oxygen Consumption.

2 Use of anaerobic exercise; need to repay oxygen not used.

3 Remove lactic acid.

Page 22

1 Increased heart rate; increased breathing rate; increased temperature.

2 Tiredness/fatigue; nausea/light-headedness; aching/DOMS/cramp.

3 Delayed onset muscle soreness; aching muscles day after strenuous exercise.

4 Strenuous/different exercise/eccentric contractions; tiny muscle tears releasing fluids.

Page 24

1 Water/minerals/carbohydrates.

2 Flush out waste/lactic acid; reduce swelling.

3 Slowly reduce heart rate and breathing rate; relaxes muscles; removes lactic acid.

Page 25

1 Loss of weight; increased muscle/hypertrophy.

2 Hypertrophy; stronger contractions – increased stroke volume; reduced resting heart rate/bradycardia.

3 Increased stamina; strength; speed; suppleness; muscular endurance.

Practice questions

Page 20

Aerobic; uses oxygen; long distance/duration; low intensity;

Glucose + oxygen = energy + water + carbon dioxide.

Page 21

Extra oxygen required; after exercise; to maintain high breathing rate and temperature/remove CO_2.

Page 21

Your heart beats stronger and faster/stroke volume increases.

Your breathing quickens and deepens/tidal volume increases.

Your body temperature increases.

You start to sweat/go red.

Page 22

a) Build up of lactic acid; excess fluids.

b) Tiny tears in muscles; excess fluids.

Page 24

Jogging/walking/easy movements; (static) stretching.

Page 25

a) Stamina, muscular endurance; speed; strength suppleness/flexibility.

b) Change in body shape; increased stroke volume/hypertrophy; reduced resting heart rate/bradycardia.

Activity

Page 20

- Aerobic – marathon, triathlon (possibly cricket).
- Anaerobic – pole vault, trampolining.
- Mixed – netball, cricket, (possibly pole vault).

Page 20

For example, football

Aerobic– standing during break in play, walking to retrieve ball, jogging when not in possession.

Anaerobic – sprinting into space, jumping up to head ball, shooting at goal.

Page 21

Tired due to production of lactic acid from anaerobic exercise.

During recovery EPOC occurs and oxygen is used to remove the lactic acid.

Page 21

- Heart beats faster.
- Breathing rate increases.
- Body temperature increases.

Page 22

- Fatigue
- Dizzy/lightheaded
- Nausea/feeling sick
- Delayed onset muscle soreness (DOMS)

Page 24

- Cool down
- Ice baths
- Massage

Page 25

- 1st activity
- HR = 4
- HR = 3

Page 25

- Muscular strength – anaerobic, moving heavy objects/weights
- Muscular endurance – anaerobic repeated exercises
- Suppleness/flexibility – repeated movements
- Speed – rapid anaerobic exercises
- Stamina – rhythmical aerobic exercises

Chapter 2 Movement analysis

Check your understanding

Page 30

1 Third class lever.

2 First class lever.

3 Second class lever.

4 Moves heavy weight; permits large force to be applied.

Page 31

1 Isotonic – movement occurs; isometric – static/no movement.

2 Concentric – muscle shortens; eccentric – muscle lengthens.

3 Gymnast balancing; athlete/swimmer on starting blocks; weight-lifter holding finishing position; wicketkeeper waiting for delivery.

Page 33

1 Sagittal plane and transverse axis.

2 Transverse plane and longitudinal axis.

3 Frontal plane and sagittal axis.

Page 34

1 Latissimus dorsi.

2 Extension.

3 Eccentric; triceps.

Page 35

1 Plantar flexion – toes pointed by action of gastrocnemius; dorsiflexion – toes pulled up by action of tibialis anterior.

2 Joint action – extension; agonist – quadriceps.

3 Muscle contraction – eccentric; agonist – quadriceps.

Page 36

1 Flexion and abduction.

2 Frontal plane and sagittal axis.

3 Rotation.

Page 37

1

	TYPE OF CONTRACTION	MAIN AGONIST	JOINT ACTION
Upward phase	Concentric	Triceps	Extension
Downward phase	Eccentric	Triceps	Flexion

Page 38

1

	TYPE OF CONTRACTION	MAIN AGONIST	JOINT ACTION
Hip	Concentric	Hip flexor	Flexion
Knee	Concentric	Quadriceps	Extension
Ankle	Concentric	Gastrocnemius	Plantar flexion

2 Joint action – plantar flexion; type of contraction – isometric.

3 Knee – flexion; ankle – dorsiflexion.

Page 40

1 Transverse plane; longitudinal axis.

2

	TYPE OF CONTRACTION	MAIN AGONIST	JOINT ACTION
Upward phase	Concentric	Quadriceps	Extension
Downward phase	Eccentric	Quadriceps	Flexion

3

	TYPE OF CONTRACTION	MAIN AGONIST	JOINT ACTION
Upward phase	Concentric	Gastrocnemius	Plantar flexion
Downward phase	Eccentric	Gastrocnemius	Dorsiflexion

Practice questions

Pages 40–41

1 **A** – isometric; **B–C** – isotonic.

2 **a)** agonist – triceps; antagonist – biceps
b) position **A** – isometric; **A** to **B** – eccentric
c) sagittal plane and transverse axis.

3 **a)** **(i)** Flexion
(ii) Flexion
b) Agonist – biceps; type of contraction – concentric/isotonic
c) Transverse plane and longitudinal axis.

Activity

Page 29

Page 30

Chapter 3 Physical training

Check your understanding

Page 43

Health is a state of complete physical, mental and social well-being and not merely the absence of disease or infirmity.

Fitness is the ability to meet/cope with the demands of the environment.

Page 44

Answers should provide a reasoned conclusion which links the ability to change direction at speed to the demands of the sports chosen, for example in football where players need to outmanoeuvre opponents, or tennis, where players may need agility to react to their opponent's shot.

Page 45

Balance is maintaining the centre of mass over the base of support.

The two types of balance are: static and dynamic.

Page 46

Cardio-vascular endurance is the ability of the heart and lungs to supply oxygen to the working muscles.

Co-ordination is the ability to use two or more body parts together smoothly and efficiently.

Page 47

Flexibility is the range of movement possible at a joint.

Muscular endurance is the ability of a muscle or group of muscles to undergo repeated contractions avoiding fatigue.

Page 48

Power is strength x speed.

Speed is the maximum rate at which an individual is able to perform a movement or cover a distance.

Page 49

Strength is the ability to overcome a resistance.

Page 59

Refer to the test protocols referred to on pages 51–59.

Page 62

The principles of training: specificity, progressive overload, reversibility, tedium.

The principles of overload: frequency, intensity, time, type.

Page 69

HIIT training is periods of extreme intensity with periods of rest.

Page 71

Static stretching is when a stretch is held (isometrically) for 30 seconds.

Advantages include: increase in range of movement at a joint, easily completed, relatively safe.

Disadvantages include: time consuming, some muscles easier to stretch than others, can lead to injury (over-stretching).

Page 72

Strength is high weight/low reps, muscular endurance is low weight/high reps.

Practice questions

Page 43

Be less likely to catch some illnesses or disease.

Page 46

10,000 m would require cardio-vascular endurance as it:
- is of long duration
- requires oxygen/use of the aerobic energy system.

Page 50

1   Yes it is needed for netball (changing direction at speed) so that the player can dodge or move into space or stay with and mark opponents.

2   Any sporting example that requires reaction to a stimulus, e.g. reacting to the gun in sprinting. Answer must contain two elements:
- the stimulus
- the time taken to start to initiate the movement.

3   Muscular endurance is not needed.

4   Balance can be static (still) or dynamic (whilst moving).
- It is the ability to maintain the centre of mass over the base of support.
- It is needed in team games – static, e.g. to hold a position ready to take a set shot in basketball (or any other suitably static example).
- It is needed in team games – dynamic, e.g. when dribbling a football.

5 The maximum rate at which an individual is able to perform a movement or cover a distance in a period of time. Distance divided by time. Needed to find space, sprint for a lost ball, to track an opponent, etc.

6 To overcome the resistance from another player to hold someone off/shield the ball/to apply force into a tackle, etc.

7 Reference to any non-enduring activity with reasoned justification why cardio-vascular endurance is not needed.

Page 60

1 Cones, 20 m tape measure, CD of text, record sheet.

2 Any two from:
- To identify strengths and/or weaknesses in a performance. Are there reasons for performing well or not so well? E.g. perhaps your dribbling in a hockey match was poor because of a lack of speed?
- To inform your training requirements – as a result of initial tests, what components did you score poorly in and therefore may need to improve?
- To show a starting level of fitness. By testing at the start of a training programme, you can work out what level you are starting at.
- To monitor improvement. Have the components of fitness you needed to improve actually improved over a period of time?
- To gauge the success of a training programme. If you have been training specific components of fitness you may well test how well it has gone by undertaking fitness tests.
- To compare against norms of the group/national averages. You can compare results with your peers or for an informed appraisal. Some tests have national averages that you can compare your scores to.
- To motivate/set goals. Having knowledge that you will be doing fitness tests may well motivate an individual to try harder or to train in advance of the test so as to score well. It could also be that an individual is set a specific goal to achieve in the tests, thus providing them with motivation (drive).
- To provide variety to a training programme. Training programmes can be boring and lack variety. Carrying out tests either randomly or on a planned basis may well provide the variety required to keep individuals enthused and motivated.

3 Any two from:
- Tests are often not sport specific and can be too general. For example, the ruler drop test is not something that is carried out in any sport.
- They do not replicate movements of activities – very few sports involve direct running of 20 m up and down in a straight line like the multi-stage fitness test.
- They do not replicate competitive conditions required in sports – major sporting events are performed under extreme pressure. Many of the tests can be repeated/retried.
- Many of the tests have questionable reliability. As most tests are maximal, the individual must try their hardest in the test to gain

an accurate score, thus motivation levels must be high. Also, as a partner sometimes measures your score, e.g. vertical jump test, it is possible that they will get the scoring wrong.

- The tests must be carried out with the correct procedures and protocols, otherwise scores will not be accurate or valid.

4 Yes, because netball needs opponents to change direction at speed, in order to dodge, lose or mark opponents, etc. It is a vital component of fitness for a netball player.

5

- Equipment: appropriate weights/resistance machine – usually a bar bell or bench press machine.
- Lift a weight once using the correct technique.
- If completed attempt a heavier weight until the heaviest weight the individual can possibly lift once is discovered (one correctly completed repetition).
- If a weight cannot be lifted, a lighter weight should be used to calculate the maximum weight that can be lifted.

Page 61

1 A measurement which has been quantified as a number, e.g. time in seconds, or goals scored. There is no opinion expressed (qualitative). It is a fact. It is often the case that quantitative scores in fitness tests can be compared to national averages.

Page 63

1 Frequency means how often you train.

2 Progressive overload:
- working harder than normal
- whilst gradually and sensibly increasing the intensity of training.

3 Make the training:
- specific to the activity
- specific to the movements used
- specific to the muscles used
- specific to the energy systems used.

Page 65

1 Consider fitness aim, fitness level, number of stations, work/rest ratio, equipment available, space available, etc.

2 The amount of work done at a station compared to the rest in between stations.

Page 67

1 It would benefit any performer whose sport is enduring/long in duration, e.g. marathon runner, long distance runner, cyclist, games player.

2 60–80 per cent of 220 − age.

3 It is not appropriate:
- not an aerobic event
- is an anaerobic event
- does not need cardio-vascular endurance.

4 Speed play. Altering the intensity/speed/terrain to improve cardio-vascular endurance. Can improve aerobic and anaerobic systems.

Page 69

1 HIIT training is periods of extreme intensity with periods of rest.

2 Advantages (any 2 of):
- Burns body fat and calories quickly.
- Can be altered easily to suit the individual.
- Can be completed relatively quickly.
- Can improve the anaerobic and aerobic energy systems.

Page 71

1 Any two from:
- stretching to the limit
- holding the stretch (isometrically) for approximately 30 seconds
- avoiding over stretching as injury can occur
- using the correct technique, e.g. avoid dangerous stretches such as straight legged toe touches
- by making the stretches appropriate to the sport
- by making sure the muscles stretched are used in the sport

2 Stretches should make use of muscles/muscle groups used within the sport.

Page 73

1 Muscular endurance – less than 70 per cent of one rep max. Three sets of 12–15 reps.

2 Any sport that is explosive/powerful, e.g. shot, discus, javelin, etc. Weights can increase the strength in targeted muscles used during performance.

Page 75

1 No. Sprinting is an anaerobic sport. Altitude training is for endurance athletes who use oxygen.

2 Any three from:
- It can be very difficult to complete training. Some people find it too hard and actually train less than if they were at sea level.
- This means that fitness can actually be lost.
- Some athletes can suffer from altitude sickness – a feeling of nausea.
- The benefits are lost quite quickly – i.e. when returning to sea level, red blood cell count starts to decrease again.

Page 75

To rest/recover/do light aerobic work to prevent loss of fitness.

Page 77

1 Warm up should include:
- gradual pulse-raising activity, e.g. fast walk/ jog/ light swim
- stretching – of all relevant muscles
- skill-based practices/familiarisation activities, e.g. ball work in football
- mental preparation – starting to get focused, using techniques to control arousal, e.g. deep breathing.

2 Benefits of cooling down.
- It allows the body to start to recover after exercising.
- It helps with the removal of lactic acid, carbon dioxide and waste products.
- It can help to prevent the delayed onset of muscle soreness, sometimes referred to as DOMS.

Activity

Page 44

EXAMPLE SPORTING SCENARIO	JUSTIFICATION
Rugby player	Needs to change direction to avoid a tackler or to perform a side-step
Hockey player	To avoid opponents perhaps using an Indian dribble manoeuvre into shooting or passing position
Badminton player	If the shuttle unexpectedly clips the net or if the player is moving one way and the shuttle is hit back the other
Dancer	To make use of the space available or to change shape and direction into a new move or to express emotion

Page 45

GYMNASTIC EXAMPLE	TYPE OF BALANCE	JUSTIFICATION
Handstand	Static	Position of handstand has to be held whilst maintaining control, e.g. no wobbles
Headstand	Static	Position of headstand has to be held for several seconds whilst maintaining control, e.g. no wobbles
Cartwheel along a beam	Dynamic	Moving along the beam without falling off. Maintain control during the jump/ rotation/movement
Tumble	Dynamic	Carrying out the tumble/ somersaults without losing control. Movement must flow, e.g. look controlled and joined together

Page 45

Basketball is a game with 4 quarters, which each last for 12 minutes (a total of 48 minutes), thus cardio-vascular endurance is needed. Most of the game requires the use of oxygen – the aerobic energy system.

Page 48

10 metres per second.

Page 72

Use less than 70 per cent of 50 kg and lift 3 sets of approximately 15 reps.

Chapter 4 Sport psychology

Check your understanding

Page 80

Skills are learned whereas abilities are inherited and stable.

Page 81

Basic skills can be done by beginners. They can be taught quickly and involve little thinking/decision making. Complex skills involve much decision making and can usually only be done by experts.

Page 82

Open skills are affected by the environment and can change as a result of, for example, opposition players. Closed skills are unaffected by the environment and are repeatable each time.

Page 83

Self-paced skills are controlled by you. You control how fast or quickly you move. Externally-paced skills are as a result of external factors, e.g. having to run to keep up with an opponent you are marking.

Page 83

Gross skills involve large muscle groups and big movements which are not precise. Fine skills involve small muscle groups and precise movements.

Page 85

Performance goals involve comparison to yourself, e.g. to beat a personal best, whereas outcome goals refer to the actual outcome, e.g. to win.

Page 88

Input, decision making, output, feedback.

Page 90

Beginners need visual and perhaps some verbal and manual/mechanical guidance.

Elite performers tend to need verbal more than visual.

Page 94

Arousal is a physical and mental (physiological and psychological) state of alertness/excitement varying from deep sleep to intense excitement.

Page 95

Answers must link the level of arousal required to the chosen skills.

Page 96

Somatic is using the body, e.g. deep breathing. Mental is controlled inside your head using thoughts/the mind, e.g. mental rehearsal.

Page 97

Direct aggression is when there is actual physical contact between performers. The 'aggressor' uses physical contact to directly and deliberately inflict harm upon their opponent.

Indirect aggression does not involve physical contact. The aggressive act is taken out on an object to gain an advantage over an opponent.

Page 99

A person with an introvert personality does not need a high level of arousal. They can become over aroused when over stimulated. They are shy/quiet/ thoughtful/loner/happy in their own company/tend to play individual sports.

A person with an extrovert personality needs a high level of arousal. They can lack concentration and often seek exciting situations, e.g. team sports.

Page 100

Motivation is the drive to succeed or the desire (want) to achieve something.

Practice questions

Page 82

1 Skills are learned and when mastered are consistently done in a way that looks easy and with the right technique.

Abilities are inherited. They are known as 'traits', which remain fairly stable during your life

2 • A shot in football during open play is an open skill. It is affected by the changing environment, e.g. you may try to bend it round defenders, hit it with the laces to exert power past a diving goalkeeper. Your choice of what type of shot to use depends on factors in the environment.

• A volley in volleyball is an open skill. You may alter the way you perform a volley because of changing factors in the environment, e.g. team mates who move/change position, the movement and positioning of the opposition, etc.

• A forward roll in gymnastics is a closed skill. It is not affected by a changing environment or people around you. You try to repeat the same action each time.

• A high jump is a closed skill. It is not affected by a changing environment or people around you. You try to repeat the same action each time.

• A goalkeeper trying to save a penalty flick in hockey is an open skill. This is because the action of saving the ball may be different depending upon what the opponent does. You may need to save low or high, left or right, with feet or with stick depending on the penalty taker. Thus it is affected by the environment.

Page 83

A javelin throw is a gross skill. The performer uses large muscle groups to run and throw the javelin.

Page 85

A COMPLETE BEGINNER PLAYING BADMINTON AGAINST A MORE EXPERIENCED PLAYER	Performance goal: To hit the shuttle more consistently than the last game	Outcome goal: To score a point
AN ELITE LEVEL JAVELIN THROWER PERFORMING AT THE OLYMPIC GAMES	Performance goal: To beat their personal best throw	Outcome goal: To win gold

Page 88

1 Selective attention involves choosing the most appropriate sense/information/cue at that time and discarding the others.

2 Input:

- Performer takes in information from the display (senses – sight, hearing, etc.).
- They choose which sense is the most important to them at that time.

E.g. sight when watching a cricket ball flying through the air. This is called selective attention, i.e. attending to the most relevant sense.

Page 90

Visual could be a coach's demonstration or video/DVD (or equivalent).

Verbal guidance could come from a coach's feedback, a parent or peer.

Manual/mechanical could involve a coach guiding the player's arm through the movement of e.g. a shot.

Page 93

1 Visual guidance.

2 It can demotivate them/cause them to stop/not persevere.

3 Knowledge of results. They are unable to understand the performance completely but can interpret the outcome, e.g. you hit the ball.

Page 94

As arousal increases so does performance.

Up to the optimal level/point.

If arousal increases further performance will decrease.

Page 97

1 Self-talk OR mental rehearsal.

2 Deep breathing is a physical (somatic) technique which involves the performer exaggerating their breaths in and out.

Page 98

Direct – physical contact has been used to deliberately hurt the opponent.

Page 99

Usually shy.

Page 100

1 Motivation is the drive to succeed or the desire (want) to achieve something. Intrinsic motivation is the drive that comes from within the performer themselves.

2 Extrinsic motivation is the drive experienced by a performer when striving to achieve a reward (tangible or intangible).

3 Intrinsic is more powerful because: overuse of extrinsic can undermine intrinsic value. You are more likely to persist if motivated intrinsically. Effort is more likely to be sustained if intrinsically motivated. Performers can become too reliant of extrinsic motivation.

Activity

Page 81

A forward roll is a basic skill. It requires little or no decisions to be made to ensure it is successful. It is often taught to beginners.

A double somersault is a complex skill. It requires decisions to be made such as how much tuck to have or when to open out so that the performer can land safely.

Page 83

- A javelin throw is self-paced. The performer chooses when to start the run up and how fast to run.
- A sprint start is externally paced. The sprinter decides to start because of the gun (external source).
- A conversion (kick) in rugby is self-paced. The rugby player starts his/her run up to take the kick when they want to.

Page 85

S – Specific (to the demands of the sport/muscles used/movements involved).

M – Measureable (it must be possible to measure whether they have been met).

A – Accepted (it must be accepted/agreed by the performer and the performer's coach – if they have one).

R – Realistic (it must actually be possible to complete the goal, i.e. they are physically capable).

T – Time-bound (it must be set over a fixed period of time).

Page 86

Answers must apply the stages of input, decision making, output and feedback, making reference to the demands of the chosen skill.

Page 93

BEGINNER	WHO REQUIRES THE FOLLOWING AND WHY?	ELITE PERFORMER
Definitely need visual guidance to understand what a skill looks like	Visual guidance?	Are unlikely to need visual guidance other than to highlight minor faults, e.g. use of slow motion
Also need verbal guidance but it should not be too long or complex	Verbal guidance?	Will need verbal guidance. It is likely to be longer and more complex than that given to a beginner. It allows 'fine-tuning' of technique
Are also likely to need manual/mechanical guidance to support or guide through the correct technique	Manual/mechanical guidance?	Elite performers are unlikely to need manual/mechanical guidance unless there is an unexpected flaw in technique
May be demotivated by negative feedback	Positive or negative feedback?	More accepting of negative feedback
Cannot interpret complex feedback on performance	Knowledge of results or performance?	Elite performers can interpret complex feedback on performance
Cannot provide themselves with feedback	Extrinsic or intrinsic feedback?	Can provide themselves with feedback

Page 96

SPORTING SITUATION	AROUSAL LEVEL	DO THEY NEED TO CONTROL/ ADJUST THEIR AROUSAL LEVEL?	IF YES, SUGGEST AN APPROPRIATE TECHNIQUE
Archery	Medium	Yes – it should be low for a fine skill	Any of: deep breathing (physical) mental rehearsal/ visualisation/ imagery (mental) positive self-talk (mental)
Weightlifter	High	No – it should be high	Not applicable
Snooker player	High	Yes – it should be low for a fine skill	Any of: deep breathing (physical) mental rehearsal/ visualisation imagery (mental) positive self-talk (mental)

Page 98

ACTIVITY	DIRECT OR INDIRECT?
A tennis player smashes a return	Indirect – no contact
A sailor cuts across an opponent's sailing line	Indirect – no actual contact
A netball player deliberately sticks her elbows out to catch an opponent's face	Direct – physical contact
A hockey player tackles an opponent, swiping their legs with their stick	Direct – physical contact

Page 99

INTROVERT		EXTROVERT
Pistol shooting		
Shy		
		Seek excitement
		Rugby player
Snooker player		
Calm		
		Sociable

Chapter 5a Socio-cultural influences

Check your understanding

Page 104

1 Participation levels of different groups of people.

2 Fixed, simplified ideas about a group/person.

3 Afro-Caribbean; Pakistani; Indian; Bangladeshi; Black African; Somali; many others.

4 Low disposable income; expectation of domestic work; fewer opportunities; low media coverage, etc.

Page 105

1 Role models; media coverage; low cost to participate; others.

2 Accepted role within culture; socio-economics; lack of role models/media coverage; low status in culture; clothing/cultural restrictions; others.

3 Young people – participation will be high; because of compulsory PE in schools; young people post-school – there is a large dropout; young people tend to play team games; older people will have lower levels of participation; older people's participation tends to be in individual activities.

Page 107

1 Disabled individuals performing with able-bodied individuals.

2 Unjust or prejudicial treatment of different categories of people.

3 Sensory, motor and mental impairments.

4 Reduced discrimination, less stereotyping, fewer barriers.

Page 109

1 Opinions about people and things.

2 Television (terrestrial cable and satellite), radio, newspapers, magazines, internet.

3 Change start times/seasons/rules; reduces attendances/participation; only major sports; sensationalise.

Page 112

1 Lack of facilities; lack of disposable income; lack of role models; negative attitudes.

2 Family commitments; lack of familiarity with activity; sexism lack of leisure time.

3 Increased media coverage; increased ease of access/more opportunities; education/health reasons; role models etc.

Practice questions

Page 103

Yes:

- Women have more leisure time/less tied to home/housework. Women have greater disposable income/greater mobility/accessibility to transport.

- Women encouraged to participate on the grounds of health/fitness/weight loss.

Promoted by the media/fashionable activity/role model.

Improvement in childcare facilities/creches/allows for more opportunities.

Positive discrimination by local leisure centres to encourage women's participation/women only sessions.

No:

Lack of equal opportunities/male-dominated sports.

Rules/regulations/preventing women/girls playing with/against men.

Sexual harassment/verbal abuse discourages participation.

Sexual stereotyping channelling girls/women into female appropriate sports.

Less tournament earnings, e.g. Wimbledon/lack of media coverage.

Page 105

Stereotype/lower expectations by society;

Self-perception/low self-esteem/inferior/less confident;

Lack of specialised coaches/trained staff;

Lack of specialist/adapted/suitable or equivalent facilities/access ramps;

Discrimination;

Lack of competition/clubs;

Lack of mobility/transport/personal income;

Lack of information/poor media coverage/ lack of role models.

Page 107

Treating people differently/unfairly through prejudice;

Based on stereotyping;

Illegal in UK.

Page 107

Stereotyping – shared image/simplistic generalisations/judgement of a group of people.

Inclusiveness – including all kinds of people/everyone within an activity or group.

Page 112

Any four from:

Stereotyping/lower expectations by society/discrimination;

Self-perception/low self-esteem/feel inferior/less confident;

Lack of specialised coaches/trained staff;

Lack of specialist/adapted/suitable or equivalent facilities/access ramps;

Lack of mobility/transport/personal income;

Lack of information/poor media coverage/lack of role models.

Activity

Page 107

Wheelchair athletics, wheelchair rugby, wheelchair tennis, wheelchair basketball, wheelchair fencing, seated volleyball, seated shooting, seated archery, visually impaired football, goalball, cycling

Page 110

EVENT	WOMEN	MEN
Football World Cup	2015 Third Place	2014 Group stages
Rugby World Cup	2014 Winners	2015 Group stages
Cricket World Cup	2013 Quarter Finals	2015 Group stages

Page 112

Family commitments, lack of leisure time, lack of familiarity with activity, lack of sufficient knowledge through education, socio-economic factors, lack of disposable income.

Chapter 5b Commercialisation of physical activity and sport

Check your understanding

Page 115

1 Using sport as a way of selling and buying goods.
2 Sport/spectators; sponsors/business; media.
3 Providing goods/money in exchange for publicity.
4 Publicity; association; support; tax deductible.

Page 118

1 TV, newspapers, magazines, radio, internet, social media.
2 Provide detailed information/statistics.
3 Broadsheet; tabloid.

Page 120

1 Provide clothing; equipment; footwear; transport; facilities; food/drink.
2 Invasion of privacy; time taken up; loss of sponsorship; negativity linked to product.
3 Affect timings; affect what/who is shown; interfere with viewing experience/adverts; repeated breaks/time-outs; change rules/format.
4 Benefits – increased income; fame; travel. Disadvantages – increased criticism; loss of privacy.

Page 121

1 More matches; more informed; better standards; better facilities.
2 Cost; isolation from performers; lack of interaction.
3 Huge audience; exciting activity; winning; lots of publicity; sponsor's name on TV; increased sales, etc.

Page 123

1 Benefit – accurate decisions; disadvantage – time wasted waiting.
2 Improved nutrition; fitness; training; recovery; safety; equipment, etc.
3 Time wasted; unfair due to cost/not for everybody.

Page 125

1 Better/accurate decisions; accurate measurements; better equipment/performances/facilities/clothing/footwear; more informed spectators.

2 Time consuming; stops flow of game; decisions still matter of opinion.

3 Better advertising; better spectacle; more matches/opportunities, etc.

Practice questions

Page 114

1 Media uses sport to gain viewers/readers; media used by business for advertising; business pays for media advertising space/time; business pays sport to act as advertising medium; sport must be in media to attract sponsorship.

2 **Benefits to sport**: Sport gets money for allowing events to be televised; business pays sports for advertising at grounds/events/sponsorship; sport becomes popularised/more fans. **Disadvantages to sport**: media sensationalise sport/reports dysfunctional aspects; media affects organisation/timing of sport; media can change nature of sport/breaks/length/method; only popular sports televised; business – players spend too much time working/appearances; business – more pressure to win due to sponsorship pressure.

Page 118

- New competitions/formats introduced.
- Playing times/seasons altered.
- Ticket allocations given to sponsors, not fans.
- More popular sports gain more coverage at expense of minority sports.
- Fewer viewers for some sports due to pay-per-view/subscription channels.
- Lower attendance at events that are televised.

Page 121

- Increased money/sponsorship.
- Performers become well known/role models.
- Increased participation/increased spectators.
- Money for better facilities/equipment/training/coaches.
- Performers able to train full time.
- Increase in number of events/competitions.

Page 125

- Ensure correct decisions are made.
- Use of Hawkeye/TMO.
- Officials communicate with each other.
- Timing/measurement accurate.

Chapter 5c Ethical issues

Check your understanding

Page 127

1 Unwritten rules about behaviour during sport.

2 Shake hands after match; not arguing with referee; not appealing for a throw; returning ball to opposition for free kicks, etc.

3 Bending, but not breaking rules to gain advantage.

4 Unwritten agreement to play by the rules to the best of your ability and to let opponent do the same.

Page 130

1 To mask pain; delay fatigue; increase alertness.

2 Power/strength athletes.

3 Low blood pressure; loss of concentration; coma.

Page 131

1 Increased red blood cells/better oxygen transport.

2 Reduce/flush out water content.

3 Endurance performer/marathon runner/cyclist.

4 Drug that reduces effects of adrenaline.

Page 131

1 Increased fame; income; status; everybody is on level playing field.

2 Cheating; bans; fines; loss of reputation; health risk.

3 Loss of reputation; credibility; income/sponsorship.

Page 132

1 Increased income – better players/facilities; creates atmosphere.

2 Most results are wins for home team/loses for away team.

3 Violent, destructive behaviour by football fans.

Page 134

1 Increased pressure; hooliganism; safety costs;

2 Reduced participation; rivalries; media hype; alcohol; gang culture; frustration; display of masculinity.

3 Early kick-offs; all-seater stadiums; segregation of fans. Improved security; alcohol restrictions; banning troublemakers; campaigns/role models.

Practice questions

Page 127

Bad sportsmanship; it's a form of cheating; trying to get a free-kick; against the rules.

Page 127

Penalties within/after the event – bookings/free kicks/sin bin;

Fair play awards/allocation of place in major event based on disciplinary record;

Clubs fined/points deducted;

Matches played behind closed doors/spectators banned from watching;

Fair play charters/code of conduct/campaigns;

Drug testing.

Page 130

Increase numbers of red blood cells; better oxygen transport; endurance performers.

Page 130

Increase muscle mass; speed up recovery; train more frequently/intensely.

Page 131

Advantages – Increased fame; income; status; everybody is on level playing field.

Disadvantages – Cheating; bans; fines; loss of reputation; health risk.

Page 134

(a) Early kick-offs; all-seater stadiums; segregation of fans; improved security; alcohol restrictions; bannig troublemakers; campaigns/role models.

(b) Rivalries; media hype; alcohol; gang culture; frustration; display of masculinity.

Activity

Page 130

EFFECTS ON ATHLETE	TYPE OF PED	SPORT THAT MIGHT BENEFIT
Enhance alertness	Stimulant	Sprinting
Reduce heart rate	Betablockers	Archery
More red blood cells/ better oxygen transport	EPO	Cycling
Mask drug use	Diuretics	Any drug-taker
Increased muscle strength/power/recovery time	Anabolic agents	Weight-lifting
Mask pain	Narcotic analgesic	Football

Page 130

Advantages – better performance, success, fame, income, level playing field

Disadvantages – cheating, bans, fines, loss of reputation, health risks

Chapter 6 Health and fitness

Check your understanding

Page 136

Health: A state of complete physical, mental and social well-being and not merely the absence of disease or infirmity.

Fitness: The ability to meet/cope with the demands of the environment.

Well-being: A mix of physical, social and mental well-being that give people a sense of *being* comfortable, healthy, and/or happy.

Page 138

Wearing a team strip provides not only clothing but also a sense of belonging; a team strip suggests friendship and support as well as some value in society and social activity.

Page 141

Some potential consequences of choosing to have a sedentary lifestyle are: gaining weight/becoming obese, suffering from heart disease, hypertension, diabetes, poor sleep or insomnia. Also can suffer from poor self-esteem or self-confidence, feeling tired or lethargic, and could have a lack of friends, poor communication skills.

Page 147

Ectomorph – tall, thin, low fat content.

Endomorph – pear shaped, high fat content.

Mesomorph – thin waist, high muscle content, wedge shaped.

Page 148

Male 2500 kcal, female 2000 kcal.

Page 150

Seven classes of food: carbohydrate, fat, protein, fibre, vitamins, minerals, water.

Balanced diet: eating the right amount (for energy expended)/the right amount of calories, according to how much you exercise. Eating different food types to provide suitable nutrients, vitamins and minerals.

Page 153

1   55-60 per cent carbohydrate, 25-30 per cent fat, and 15-20 per cent protein.

2   Vitamins and minerals are for maintaining the efficient working of the body systems and general health.

3   Dehydration: excessive loss of body water interrupting the function of the body. Hydration: having enough water (water balance) to enable normal functioning of the body. Rehydration: consuming water to restore hydration.

Practice questions

Page 139

1   Social health and well-being: a state of complete physical, mental and social well-being and not merely the absence of disease or infirmity. Mental health and well-being: the ability to meet or cope with the demands of the environment. Physical health and well-being: a 'feel-good' chemical released during exercise.

2   Health: a state of complete physical, mental and social well-being and not merely the absence of disease or infirmity. Fitness: the ability to meet or cope with the demands of the environment.

3   All body systems working well.

Page 141

1   Sedentary lifestyle is choosing to take part in little or no exercise.

2   (Any three of the following):

   ● gaining weight/becoming obese (physical health and well-being)

   ● suffering from heart disease (physical health and well-being)

   ● suffering from hypertension (physical health and well-being)

   ● suffering from diabetes (physical health and well-being)

   ● suffering from poor sleep/insomnia (physical health and well-being)

   ● suffering from poor self-esteem/confidence (mental health and well-being)

   ● feeling tired and lethargic (physical/mental health and well-being)

   ● having a lack of friends/poor communication skills (social health and well-being).

Page 143

1 Obesity is a term used to describe people with a large fat content – caused by an imbalance of calories consumed to energy expenditure. BMI of over 30 or 20 per cent or more above ideal weight for height.

One of the following:

- Can lead to depression.
- Can cause a loss of confidence.
- Can make the individual feel like they can't contribute to society (well-being).

2 One of the following:

- Limit stamina/cardio-vascular endurance – thus making it difficult to perform any activities of a long duration.
- Limit flexibility – making it difficult for performers to use a full range of movement at joints when attempting to perform skills.
- Limit agility – making it difficult to change directly quickly.
- Limit speed/power – making it hard to react quickly enough or produce force.

Page 147

1 An ectomorph is tall and thin with a low fat content. They would suit an activity requiring height, e.g. high jump (or equivalent).

2 Mesomorph.

Page 150

1 Too much: the recommended daily intake is 2500 kcal for an adult male.

2 Average daily intake for a female adult is 2000 kcal. Energy is derived from food and drink intake. Training requires more energy, therefore more intake is required.

Page 153

1 No – too much fat. Justification – recommended amount is 25–30 per cent. Accept that it is OK, as long as it is linked to a factor, e.g. very tall, training a lot.

2 Any three from the following:

- The blood thickens (increased viscosity), which slows blood flow down.
- The heart rate increases which means that the heart has to work harder. This can cause an irregular heart rate (rhythm).
- The body temperature is likely to increase meaning that the body may overheat.
- Reaction time increases – in other words, it gets slower and general reactions are poorer. This of course means that decisions made may be negatively affected.
- An individual may suffer muscle fatigue and/or muscle cramps.

3 Carbohydrate is the main energy source for the body. Fat is also an energy source *at low intensity*. Protein is for growth and repair of tissues.

Activity

Page 139

TERM	DEFINITION
Health	A state of complete physical, mental and social well-being and not merely the absence of disease or infirmity
Fitness	The ability to meet/cope with the demands of the environment
Social health and well-being	Basic human needs are being met (food, shelter and clothing). The individual has friendship and support, some value in society, is socially active and has little stress in social circumstances
Mental health and well-being	A state of well-being in which every individual realises his or her own potential, can cope with the normal stresses of life, can work productively and fruitfully, and is able to make a contribution to her or his community
Physical health and well-being	All body systems working well, free from illness and injury. Ability to carry out everyday tasks
Well-being	Involves physical, mental and social well-being. It is a dynamic process of the three parts that give people a sense of being comfortable, healthy and/or happy.
Serotonin	A 'feel good' chemical released during exercise

Page 147

ACTIVITY	BODY TYPE REQUIRED
Hammer thrower	Mostly endomorph Some elements of mesomorph (muscle bulk)
Pole vaulter	Mostly ectomorph for height Some elements of mesomorph for shoulder power
400 m sprinter	Mostly mesomorph
Marathon runner	Mostly ectomorph – low fat content

Page 153

TERM	DEFINITION
Dehydration	Excessive loss of body water interrupting the function of the body
Hydration	Having enough water (water balance) to enable normal functioning of the body
Rehydration	Consuming water to restore hydration

Chapter 7 Use of data

Check your understanding

Page 155

Quantitative data involves quantities, numbers and facts. It can be collected through questionnaires or surveys.

Qualitative data involves subjective opinions gathered through interviews or observations.

Practice question

Page 155

Qualitative data – data which is subjective involving opinions relating to the quality of a performance rather than the quantity.

Quantitative data – data which can be quantified as a number, e.g. time in seconds, or goals scored. There is no opinion expressed (qualitative). It is a fact.

Page 157

(a)

(b)

Glossary

Abduction Movement where limbs are moved away from the body.

Abilities Stable inherited traits that determine individual potential to learn or acquire a skill.

Adapted sports Competitive sports for individuals with disabilities.

Adduction Movement where limbs are moved towards the body.

Adrenaline A naturally occurring hormone that prepares the body for `fight or flight'.

Aerobic exercise Exercise in the presence of/using oxygen.

Agility The ability to move and change direction quickly (at speed) while remaining in control.

Agonist The prime muscle that causes movement.

Alveoli Many tiny air sacs in the lungs which allow for rapid gaseous exchange.

Anabolic agents Drugs that help athletes to train harder and build muscle.

Anaerobic exercise Exercise in the absence of enough/ without oxygen.

Arteries Blood vessels carrying blood away from the heart.

Atria Upper chambers of the heart that collect blood from the veins.

Balance Maintaining the centre of mass over the base of support.

Ball and socket joints Joints that allow many movements.

Beta blockers Drugs which reduce the effects of adrenaline on the body.

Blood doping Artificially increasing the number of red blood cells in the blood.

Bradycardia Lowered resting heart rate due to long-term exercise.

Bronchi Tubes that carry air from the trachea to the lungs.

Capillaries Very thin blood vessels that allow gas exchange to happen.

Carbohydrates Food sources which act as the body's preferred energy source.

Cardiac cycle Sequence of events that occur when the heart beats.

Cardio-vascular endurance The ability of the heart and lungs to supply oxygen to the working muscles.

Co-ordination The ability to use different (two or more) parts of the body together smoothly and efficiently.

Contract to compete Agreeing to play by the rules, trying to win, but also allowing your opponent to play.

Dehydration Excessive loss of body water interrupting the function of the body.

Deltoid Muscle causing flexion and some extension at the shoulder.

Diastole Term used to describe the relaxation phase of the cardiac cycle.

Discrimination The unjust or prejudicial treatment of different groups of people, especially on the grounds of race, age or sex.

Dislocation Where the bones of a joint separate from their normal position.

Disposable income Amount of income available to be spent or saved as one wishes.

Diuretics Drugs that remove fluid from the body.

DOMS (Delayed Onset Muscle Soreness) The pain/ stiffness felt in the days following strenuous exercise.

Dorsiflexion Movement at the ankle where the toes are pulled up towards the knee.

Ectomorph Individual whose body shape is tall and thin.

Embolism A blockage of a blood vessel.

Endomorph An individual with a pear-shaped body.

Engagement patterns How levels of participation vary across different social groups.

EPO (Erythropoetin) Naturally occurring substance which will increase the number of red blood cells in the body.

EPOC (Excess Post-exercise Oxygen Consumption) Increased rate of oxygen intake following strenuous activity.

Erogenic aid A technique or substance used for the purpose of enhancing performance.

Ethnic group A community made up of people who share a common cultural background.

Etiquette The unwritten rules concerning player behaviour.

Expiratory reserve volume The additional air that can be forcibly exhaled after the expiration of a normal tidal volume.

Externally-paced skills Skills controlled by external factors.

Extrinsic feedback Feedback about performance from an external source.

Extrinsic motivation The drive experienced by a performer when striving to achieve a reward.

Fat A food source that provides energy at low intensities.

First class lever Where the fulcrum lies between the effort and the resistance.

Fitness The ability to meet or cope with the demands of the environment.

Flexibility The range of movement possible at a joint.

Fulcrum The part of a lever system that pivots; joints are the fulcrum in the body's lever systems.

Gamesmanship The use of dubious methods that are not strictly legal to gain an advantage.

Golden triangle The financial relationship between sport, sponsorship and trade.

Haemoglobin The red pigment found in blood cells.

Hawkeye An optical balltracking device used as an aid to officiating in tennis and cricket.

Hinge joints Joints that allow flexion and extension.

Home-field advantage The psychological advantage that the home team has over the visiting team.

Hyperbaric chambers High pressure chambers that force oxygen into an injury to speed up recovery.

Hypertrophy The increase in the size of muscles/heart due to long-term exercise.

Information processing Using the available information in order to choose a suitable skill or movement.

Inspiratory reserve volume The additional air that can be forcibly inhaled after the inspiration of a normal tidal volume.

Integration Involving the full participation of all people in community life but usually referring to disabled people.

Interval training Training method that incorporates periods of work followed by periods of rest.

Intrinsic feedback Feedback from within the performer, for example information from the senses or muscles.

Intrinsic motivation The drive that comes from within the performer.

Isometric contraction Muscular contraction where the muscle stays the same length.

Isotonic contractions Where the muscle changes length as it contracts and causes movement of a body part.

Knowledge of performance Feedback about the quality of performance, for example technique.

Latissimus dorsi Muscle causing extension at the shoulder.

Ligaments Tissues that join bone to bone.

Long bones Bones of the legs and arms.

Manual guidance Physically moving the performer.

Match analysis Computer software that provides detailed statistical data about individual and/or team performances.

Mechanical guidance Using mechanical aids to assist a performer.

Meniscus Cartilage acting as a shock absorber between the tibia and the femur in the knee joint.

Mental rehearsal The performer pictures themselves performing the skill perfectly before attempting it.

Mesomorph An individual with a muscular appearance.

Minerals Inorganic substances which assist the body with many of its functions.

Muscular endurance The ability of a muscle or muscle group to undergo repeated contractions, avoiding fatigue.

Narcotic analgesics Painkillers that mask pain caused by injury or fatigue.

Outcome goals Judging the end result by comparison with other performers.

Oxygen debt Temporary oxygen shortage in the body due to strenuous exercise.

Oxygen (hypoxic) tents Tents that contain high oxygen concentrations to speed up recovery after injury.

Oxyhaemoglobin This is formed when oxygen combines with haemoglobin.

Peer group A group of people of approximately the same age, status and interests.

Peptide hormones Naturally occurring substances that can improve muscle growth and increase production of red blood cells.

Performance goals Personal standards to be achieved without comparison with other performers.

Philanthropic Attitudes and actions with the aim of benefiting others.

Plantar flexion Movement at the ankle where the toes are pointed towards the ground.

Prejudice Preconceived opinion that is not based on reason or actual experience.

Prosthetics Artificial aids, often replacing a limb.

Protein A food source which is predominantly for growth and repair of body tissues.

Qualitative data Data which is subjective involving opinions relating to the quality of a performance.

Quantitative data Data that can be quantified as a number, for example time in seconds or goals scored.

Residual volume The volume of air that remains in the lungs after a maximum expiration.

Resistance The load to be moved by a lever system; usually this involves weight when the body's lever systems are involved.

Role model A person looked up to by others as an example to be copied.

Rotator cuff Group of muscles causing rotation at the shoulder.

Second class lever Where the fulcrum lies at one end of the lever with the effort at the other end.

Sedentary lifestyle A person's choice to have no or little physical activity.

Self-paced skills The start of a movement is decided by the performer.

Skills A learned action or behaviour with the intention of bringing about predetermined results.

Social groups People who interact with one another, share similar characteristics and have a sense of unity or togetherness.

Somatotype A method of classifying body types.

Sponsorship Where a company pays money to a team or individual in return for advertising their goods.

Sportsmanship Appropriate, polite and fair behaviour while participating at a sporting event.

Static stretching Stretching to the limit and holding the stretch isometrically.

Steady state exercise Working continuously at the same intensity.

Stimulants Substances which make athletes more alert and mask effects of fatigue.

Synovial joints Type of joint commonly found in the limbs.

Systole Term used to describe the contraction phase of the cardiac cycle.

Television Match Official (TMO) Used in rugby union and rugby league to make decisions using replays of incidents.

Tendons Connective tissues which attach muscles to bones.

Third class lever Where the fulcrum lies at one end of the lever and the effort is in the middle.

Tidal volume The volume of air breathed in (or out) during a normal breath at rest.

Trachea Also known as windpipe. Carries air from the mouth and nose to the lungs.

Vasoconstriction Reducing the diameter of small arteries to increase blood flow to tissues.

Vasodilation Increasing the diameter of small arteries to increase blood flow to tissues.

Veins Blood vessels carrying blood towards the heart.

Ventricles Lower chambers of the heart which pump blood out of the heart to the arteries.

Verbal guidance Guidance that is provided by another person speaking to you.

Vertebrae Bones that form the spine or backbone.

Visual guidance Guidance that you can see, for example a demonstration.

Vitamins Organic substances that are required for many essential processes in the body.

Wellbeing A mix of physical, social and mental factors that give people a sense of being comfortable, healthy and/or happy.

Index